Counterfeit Justice

The True Story of 19th Century Organized Crime

To JANE,
BEST WISHES!
Eric all

Eric T. Alli

Edited by:

Megan Rachelle Shufelt and Katie Erickson

Revised by:

Barbara Thornton

Cover photo courtesy of Kristie Fox of Arlington, Ohio

ISBN: 1494822717
ISBN-13: 978-1494822712

www.facebook.com/counterfeitjustice

To my family, black sheep and all

ACKNOWLEDGMENTS

I would like to thank all of the various historians, societies, libraries, researchers, and individuals who assisted in compiling all of the information contained in this book, many of whom were volunteer. I would also like to thank my family for hearing the same stories over and over throughout the years as I was doing the research. I should also acknowledge all of those who maintained this history over the last two-hundred years so the story may be told again.

Table of Contents

1. INTRODUCTION

Imagine a criminal justice system poisoned with corrupt officials at every level. How would you cope with such a system that could not bring justice to the guiltiest in society? This was a system where the most hardened of criminals could consistently walk free with no punishment at all. The sheriff, judges, prosecutors, and everyone in between were being paid off. In today's society there are plenty of options. The system of checks and balances in the criminal justice system is far greater today than at any time in past history. In today's system, higher authorities such as the Attorney General or the Federal Bureau of Investigation would step in immediately to investigate and handle any signs of public corruption. Unfortunately for our pioneer settlers, these options were not available back then.

What if you were a pioneer settling in the Midwest where those options did not exist? Our ancestors faced this very scenario of widespread corruption during the time the Midwest was settled. Their property was being stolen regularly and their goods were being bought and sold with counterfeit money. It was not safe to travel at night. The pioneers of the Midwest dealt with intimidation, threats, arson of their property, robbery, and other violent crimes with no recourse. This became a way of everyday life for them.

The criminals involved were more than just random pockets of bandits who terrorized local communities. This was an intricate organized crime syndicate that has never been recognized in such a light. American history generally recognizes the Prohibition Era as the birth of organized crime in the United States. This is the general assumption of many in the criminal justice and academic community. However, the outfit of thieves who terrorized our pioneers was equally, if not more, organized than Al Capone, Bugs Moran, and other gangsters who operated in the 1920's and 1930's.

Almost one hundred years earlier than the gangster era, this other outfit used code words, their own language, and safe houses to conduct their operations. They used the same tactics: threats, intimidation, and sometimes even murder to achieve their goals. It was an entire network of thieves from Canada out to Iowa who were connected politically to all levels of the government, including even the President of the United States.

This is the key difference between the prohibition gangsters and those operating during the settlement of the Midwest. While there is no doubt the prohibition gangsters had their share of public officials bought and paid for at various levels, that was nothing compared to how large scale public corruption existed during the settlers' days. It was so widespread that any members of the gang who were arrested had little to worry about when it came to having justice administered. If this is the only option of a criminal justice system and that option is debauched, do you really have a criminal justice system?

Eventually the battle between good and evil in the pioneer days reached a boiling point in many communities. The pioneers took matters into their own hands. They created their own criminal justice system and used every option on the table, legal or not, to bring law and order to their small communities. It is a very dark time in American history. The settlers were tired of living in fear and suffering the loss of their property to thieves. Unsatisfied with the lack of justice, the citizens banded together and went after the criminals who had terrorized them for far too long.

In Indiana, Iowa, and other regions, the citizens banded together in companies of Regulators, citizen law enforcers who served as judge, jury, and sometimes executioner. One of the outlaws executed was a cousin of mine, a young Canadian born man named Gregor McDougall. Less than a week after his arrest, McDougall found himself hanging at the end of a rope near Ligonier, Indiana.

The tale of Gregor McDougall is a local one that has been passed along for several generations. It tells the story of a young man who took a wrong turn in life in a time long ago when Noble and Lagrange counties in Indiana were first being settled. It tells of the struggles of our ancestors to make a better life. It also exposes a series of flaws in the criminal justice system.

Although the story of McDougall and many similar tales have been passed along for generations, the facts have not always survived. Several accounts of this story have been published throughout the years. The first was written by M.H. Mott, called the "History of the Regulators," which was written from the Regulators' perspective on the events that lead to McDougall's execution. Other stories, such as "Salt and Savor" by Howard Troyer, are a mix of factual accounts and fiction.

The story did not begin or finish at the end of a rope on a cold winter afternoon in Ligonier, Indiana. It started much earlier and went on long after McDougall was executed. The true facts surrounding the McDougall execution may never be known. This incident happened in a time well before internet, cell phones, or any other modern forms of communication. As I will show, many of the sources that do still exist from that era were biased in their own way.

My interest in the McDougall execution is a story in itself. I never knew I had any relatives in Indiana until around 2001. In a strange twist, I first heard of the McDougall execution when I worked for the Wolcottville Police Department. I would regularly patrol the areas described in this book, including the infamous Tamarack area, which is now known as Frogtown. I would unknowingly patrol the cemetery where McDougall's headstone sits in the front row, without ever knowing who he was, how he got there, or that we shared the same blood. The stone reads: "GREGOR McDOUGLE" in deteriorating letters. Even his name was spelled incorrectly as a degrading postscript to his inglorious end. I suppose it is a curious charity that he was provided with a stone at all.

The goal of this book is to allow a fair review of the Blacklegs, Regulators, McDougall's life, and other events that led to his death. It is also to relate the occurrence of organized crime existing in the country long before the Prohibition Era, which challenges many previous reports. More than one hundred and fifty years after the citizen execution of McDougall, this book will allow readers to examine all of the facts in a fair manner, form an opinion, and draw their own conclusions. In essence, this book can serve as the trial McDougall and others never had. Each reader can serve on a grand jury of sorts, to decide what exactly happened in the early days of northeast Indiana and throughout the Midwest.

The story of McDougall is just one part of a larger picture. While researching McDougall, it became clear that this was much more than just a small band of thieves who settled in northeast Indiana. As I traced the story of McDougall, it quickly became clear that this band of thieves was far larger and more organized than had ever been relayed in local history books. Curiously, the history books in every region had a small mention of counterfeiters and horse thieves that plagued their area during this era. Every book would reference the members of the gang settling from another area. None of these history books ever connected all the dots.

No account of Blacklegs would be complete without mentioning the late John Martin Smith. Mr. Smith shared his fascination and knowledge of the Blacklegs and Regulators throughout the years. He was an avid collector of Regulator badges and other memorabilia from that era. Smith had a great ability to keep history alive by sharing his knowledge through his writing and speeches. It is through historians like Smith that history lives on well beyond the years any of us will spend on earth.

2. THE GODFATHER AND BEGINNINGS

A true organized crime family will have a Godfather. It is a made man who is the boss of all organized crime associates. In modern times, names such as Lucchese, Bonanno, Columbo, Genovese, and Gambino are at the top of the list. In more recent times, most will remember the infamous John Gotti. If there was a true Godfather of early organized crime in the United States, that person would be Philip Alston. Physical descriptions of Alston even bring to mind a prominent organized crime figure. Historian Otto Rothert described him as "a gentleman by birth, education, and early association. He comes down to us a handsome figure and grand in manner, wearing broad-cloth, ruffles, and lace. He had an air of chivalry to women and of aloofness, superiority, and mystery to men."

While it would be a true statement to say the overwhelming majority of Americans have never heard of Alston, he was the oldest figure who, historical evidence has shown, provided the first structure to a famous band of counterfeiters, thieves, and highway robbers that operated in the pioneer settlement days of the United States. The Sicilian mob had nothing on Alston and his associates. His ties reached across the United States to include North Carolina, Virginia, Kentucky, Ohio, Illinois, Mississippi, South Carolina, and Tennessee. It is more impressive that he was able to accomplish this in a time before any modern communication or transportation. Even before the United States issued the Declaration of Independence followed by the American Revolution, Alston began counterfeiting currency for profit. In the 1770's, authorities sought the arrest of Philip and his brother John on counterfeiting charges. By 1781, Alston became a key figure in a battle against the Spanish near Natchez, Mississippi which led to American control over that region. Though he was a key figure in this pivotal point in the region's history, he was also suspected of stealing a crucifix from the local Catholic Church at the same time. It is rumored that Alston melted down the crucifix to mint some of his own spurious coins.

Former Secretary of State and Speaker of the House Henry Clay once spoke of Philip Alston stating, "the infamy of the character of the Alstons, the old man in particular, is well known to Colonel Hart. He was long a resident of North Carolina, and I believe there was no doubt there, but besides almost every other species of crime, he counterfeited every emission of paper money which took place during his residence there." Alston's place in American history runs well beyond that of establishing the first organized crime outfit. In between his counterfeiting operations, he signed the Cumberland Compact in 1780, the original constitution for the State of Tennessee. Alston moved from Tennessee to Kentucky and settled in the area now known as Logan County. Though he was one of the pioneer settlers, it did not take long before other settlers grew tired of Alston's trade in the counterfeiting business. The other settlers banded together and banished Alston from the county altogether. It was perhaps the first act which would later start the Regulators movement. Thought not yet called Regulators, citizens banding together without the support of a criminal justice system would become commonplace in later years.

After firmly establishing himself in the role of a leader, as well as that of an outlaw criminal, Alston left Kentucky and found his way over to Hardin County, Illinois, settling in the area of Cave-in-Rock. It would be almost a century before that area would be permanently free of the syndicate's control. It was at Cave-in-Rock that Alston teamed up with John Duff, a known counterfeiter who lacked the organizational skills offered by Alston. The two men worked together to establish a nationwide network, giving Cave-in-Rock the distinguishing title for the location where organized crime was born in the United States. Most of the gang's activity in this region occurred either at Cave-in-Rock or along the Natchez Trace. It should be noted that some early references to the Blacklegs who operated in southern Illinois almost always refer to the gang as the "Flatheads." However, to remain consistent and to avoid confusion, they will be referred to as Blacklegs.

Though Alston appears to have been the Godfather, his quest for power would eventually take him away from Cave-in-Rock. He did not hold the position of boss for very long before he moved back to Tennessee. Alston is then fingered in the land scandal in Yazoo, Tennessee, which involved governors of the State of Georgia in the 1790's. They were accused of selling plots of land in an insider scheme at highly discounted prices to connected people. Alston moved from Tennessee to Mississippi, where it is believed he died.

It could be argued that John Duff was actually the Godfather. He was already settled at Cave-in-Rock upon Alston's arrival and had already inducted himself into

17

the counterfeiting trade. Duff was suspected of being a British spy and settled in that region prior to 1790. However, Alston already had a record of counterfeiting long before any records could be found on Duff, and is rumored to have been the man who brought the dies to mint coins. The other reason Alston is recognized is because of territory. Any gang or organized outfit is based upon territory. The connections Alston had to the various states, as well as having been highly mobile, draws the conclusion that he was more responsible for expansion of the operations through the middle part of the United States and into the south.

By the end of the 1790's, several other key figures would enter the picture. Samuel Mason and the Harpes, Micajah "Big" Harpe and Wiley "Little" Harpe, also arrived along with a second generation Alston. The second generation Alston is yet another reason Philip should be considered the Godfather. He was the first to bring in a second generation of criminals. Alston's son Peter involved himself in his father's operations. Peter took over counterfeiting and was also involved in the more serious crime of murder.

All of these men bring their own fascinating histories to the organized crime outfit. Samuel Mason rose through the ranks to become a Captain in the Ohio County Militia, Virginia State Forces (now West Virginia), during the American Revolution. Following the war he served as Justice of the Peace in Washington County, Pennsylvania, and served as a judge in the early days of Kentucky. The Harpes, though never leaders of the Blacklegs, had a story that was not as glamorous. Both men were suspected of being involved in the kidnapping and rape of four teenage girls in their native North Carolina. That aside, they were also believed to be involved in a series of battles serving on the side of the British. By the late 1700's the Harpes were suspected of multiple murders, including bashing the head of an infant against a tree for crying. The men continued their murderous spree by killing a man in Kentucky, followed by two other individuals traveling through from Maryland.

The first time the Harpes were brought to trial was in Knoxville, Tennessee. There they were both charged with murder and robbery, but managed to be found innocent. After relocating to Kentucky, the Harpes spent their first two years living in the woods with a group of outcast Cherokee Indians. It was in Kentucky their next murder and subsequent trial was held. The men were accused of murdering a traveler and robbing him of $2,000 in gold. After arriving in Stanford, Kentucky, the Harpes went on a spending spree which drew the attention of the locals. By the time the body of the traveler was found, the Harpes themselves were nowhere to be found. A manhunt soon began and the Harpes were found near Liberty, Kentucky in Casey County. They were both taken into custody but were soon broken out of jail and fled the area. Altogether, the Harpes were suspected in the murders of over forty people, putting both men up for the notoriety of becoming the first serial killers in the United States. Over a dozen victims were killed at Cave-in-Rock, some pushed over the cliff just so the Harpes could watch them die.

By 1799, the pioneers of the Cave-in-Rock region had enough. They had been terrorized day and night and were afraid of losing their lives if they dared to travel any distance from their homes. Into the picture rides Captain Young and his men, who gained the reputation of being "exterminators." With Young's men from Mercer County, Kentucky, they set out to rid the region of this outlaw gang. Young went after each and every one of them. In a short time over thirteen outlaws were exterminated. The most feared men, including the Harpes, managed to escape unharmed back into Kentucky and continued their crime spree.

Some of the murders appear to follow typical organized crime fashion of taking out anyone who dared to cross them. Some reports indicate that anyone who was suspected of speaking out to Young's men about their atrocities faced immediate death. Some of their victims were gutted, their bodies filled with rocks to provide weight, and were then dumped into the water. Perhaps it was the inspiration for the modern day mob version of cement shoes.

While on the run, the Harpe brothers found their way to the residence of pioneer settler James Tompkins of Steuben Lick in Henderson County, Kentucky. After sharing a meal with Tompkins and providing him with much needed gunpowder, the Harpes moved on down the road to the residence of Moses Stegall. Once the Harpes found out Stegall's wife had fifty dollars at the residence, they made plans to return for a full robbery. They killed Stegall's wife and child, as well as a guest in their house, Major William Love. Once everyone was dead the Harpes set fire to their pioneer cabin. While fleeing, the Harpes killed two other men who may have been witnesses. Not all the witnesses were gone, however. A nearby neighbor, identified as Squire McBee, was able to positively identify the Harpes as the men responsible. Moses Stegall was not at home at the time of the robbery, but quickly returned to find his whole family dead and his home in ashes. The infuriated and devastated Stegall joined the manhunt for those responsible.

The men were pursued by a heavily armed posse to Muhlenberg County, Kentucky. They were eventually found by the posse, which began a pursuit lasting over forty miles. When the pursuit finally came to a stop, the first member of the posse, James Leeper, along with John Tompkins, began negotiations with Micajah "Big" Harpe. They were soon joined by Stegall, whose only intention was to seek revenge.

After catching up with him in Muhlenberg County, Micajah "Big" Harpe was shot by either Stegall or Leeper, depending on the account. With a tomahawk, Stegall decapitated Harpe and stuck his head on a nearby sapling. The decapitated head was to serve as a warning to any other criminals in the area, though Leeper himself was suspected of once being a gang associate. For years afterward, the area was known by surveyors and mappers as "Harpe's Head, Kentucky." The location is now designated by a historical marker in Webster County.

Wiley "Little" Harpe would also meet an early death, but not before remaining on the run through 1803 using the alias John Setton. Wiley learned that there was a bounty on the head of his former associate from Cave-in-Rock, the former war hero Samuel Mason. With no honor among thieves, Wiley murdered Mason and severed his head, which he took into the village of Washington, Mississippi to claim the bounty. One of the men present to pay off on the bounty happened to be a previous victim of Harpe's robberies. Wiley was quickly arrested where a quick trial was held before Wiley's life of crime ended. He was sentenced to death and was quickly hanged on February 8, 1804.

As Samuel Mason was absent from Cave-in-Rock when the first efforts were made by the Regulators to rid of the criminal element, the organization needed leadership. The man who took over was James Wilson, who married Mason's niece. He was in charge for only a short time, but it proved long enough to establish his own mark. History notes that Wilson hung a sign over the entrance to the cave which read "Wilson's Liquor Vault and House of Entertainment." There are some who believe that Wilson and Mason were one and the same, that Mason was using the name as an alias. Finding any positive evidence of this notion would be virtually impossible.

Cave-in-Rock did not remain a peaceful place for very long following the extermination of the first gang of outlaws by Captain Young. By 1810, Azor Sturdivant, along with his father and two sons, took over operations there. The Sturdivant's originally hailed from Connecticut and Massachusetts, while their associates came from Virginia and Tennessee. They too had direct ties to service in the American Revolution. The Sturdivant's were already established members of the syndicate who brought their counterfeiting operations to Illinois from Delaware County, Ohio. By 1816, counterfeiting in Illinois became rampant. Illinois legislators passed a law during their fourth session which, in summary, stated that counterfeiters "shall suffer death by hanging, without benefit of clergy."

Ohio may be where Jim Brown and his associates met up with the Sturdivant's. However, there is other evidence to support that Brown's brother was associated with the Sturdivant's, as Daniel Brown was known for his exploits along the Ohio River which is where Cave-in-Rock is located. This was not the

Early postcard of Cave-in-Rock, Hardin County, Illinois (not in copyright)

only connection between the Browns and Sturdivant's, as we will soon find out when William Latta enters the picture.

The Sturdivant's would maintain their operations at Cave-in-Rock for slightly over a decade, but their criminal operations spanned three generations. Eventually the law abiding citizens of the region banded together in an effort to rid their home of the gang that plagued them. There would be a total of three attempts to shut down the Sturdivant's. A vigilante group of approximately forty men met at Golconda, Illinois. With the assistance of the local constable the group set off for Pope County, southwest of Cave-in-Rock, in July 1822. They were armed with warrants for the arrest of Roswell and Merrick Sturdivant.

When the Regulators raided the Blackleg hideout there were six or seven gang members hard at work manufacturing counterfeit. The upper story of the house had been converted into something of a factory, fitted with workbenches and tools used for engraving. On the floor were numerous scraps of paper cut from the ends of the fake bank notes. The raid did not last long, as word soon spread to the area that Sturdivants' shop was being raided. Merrick and Roswell were eventually taken into custody. It didn't do much good, as both would be acquitted of all charges.

The next attempt to shut the gang down occurred in 1823. During two consecutive raids over the course of several days, at least one person was shot and killed. A Blackleg with the last name of Small was shot during the first affray and died a few hours later. Leader Roswell Sturdivant was shot in the neck during the second battle aboard a steam ship named "Cincinnati," which was raided. At least one vigilante member named Rondeau was also shot and wounded in the shoulder. Roswell Sturdivant and his father were both arrested. His father would die before ever going to trial.

No sooner did the area rid itself of the Sturdivant Gang then the next group of outlaws move into the area. Known as "Ford's Ferry Gang," the group was organized and operated by James Ford, who not only served as a Sheriff and Justice of the Peace, but was also the head of the local Regulators, whose very job it was to rid the area of Ford's operation.

Ford was also the owner of a local ferry, and his gang was known to rob not only those traveling the highways, but those on the river as well. Members of the Sturdivant Gang and later the Pennington Gang have been tied to Ford, as well as the infamous Billy Potts. Once Ford was exposed as being a fraud, he became an instant target.

The beginning of the end for Ford came when he and his henchmen were involved in the murder of Vincent Simpson. At the time of his death, Simpson was employed at a ferry boat service operated by Ford. Ford and Simpson were associates, up until a civil court action ended the friendship. Ford and his men were rumored to have been responsible for numerous deaths, so it was not a problem for Ford to take out one more person. In June 1833, Simpson was murdered by a hit man working on behalf of Ford. Regulators had had enough of the violence caused by the Ford's Ferry Gang. Regulators took Ford into custody and brought him to the dock house where his ferry operated. He was tied up and given an opportunity to make his last statement. On cue, the son of Vincent Simpson squeezed the trigger of a gun placed behind Ford. The crooked sheriff and leader of the Ford's Ferry Gang was dead.

After all this violence and death at the beginning of the era of the Blackleg, the question of whatever happened to Philip Alston remains. All evidence shows that Alston lived a comfortable, affluent lifestyle as any typical Godfather would in an organized crime family. In at least one account from historian Otto Rothert, who conducted extensive research on the gang at Cave-in-Rock, Alston returned to the area of Natchez, Mississippi. Upon his return he befriended high level Spanish officials and was eventually appointed *empressidio* of Mexico. He lived the life of a mob boss, which was cut short by his untimely death.

Cave-in-Rock would continue to be the home of operations for many outlaw gangs following the days of Mason, Alston, and others. The area of Cave-in-Rock would continue to be a hotspot for criminal activity into the late 1840's. The continual battle between Regulators and outlaws resulted in casualties on both sides. Even after the Civil War, criminals were known to stay close to the region. One of those was a man named Logan Belt. Author Shadrach Jackson referred to Belt in an 1887 biography as "the most daring desperado ever known to civilization."

3. THE JAMES BROWN GANG

"Blackleg" was a term used long ago to describe criminals and frauds of all types. It is an older term, which has since been replaced by thieves, thugs, gangsters, and various other descriptions used today. Identifying the leader of the Blacklegs may be just as difficult as identifying the leader of any other organized crime family such as the Mafia. It was not a position that one would boast of publicly. As difficult as it is to identify the leaders of organized crime today, it is even more difficult to identify the leader of a gang that has not existed for over 150 years.

If a first leader of the Blacklegs in Ohio could be named, he would have been as close to a Prohibition Era gangster as could be imagined. He was described as a good looking, well-built man with deep-set eyes. He was always dressed in expensive clothing and married the daughter of a prominent family from Cleveland. His name was James 'Jim' Brown, who hailed from Boston Township in Summit County.

He should have been well dressed, as Brown was the head of one of the largest banking operations in the United States at the time. The bank had branches

*James 'Jim' Brown of Boston
Township, Summit County,
Ohio (not in copyright)*

throughout the Midwest, including Indiana and Vermont. The headquarters for his banking operation was located inside a tavern in the village of Boston, a small town near Akron. The bank headquarters is now a national historic site.

Brown built his house and store in 1825. The banking operations started in approximately 1826. The operations brought a variety of people from all over the United States to this small village. Brown was a popular individual whom few men dared to cross. Brown and his older brother Dan not only operated one of the largest banks, but also one of the most unique banks throughout American history. The financial notes provided by Jim and Dan Brown's bank were all counterfeit, and it was no secret in the community where they lived.

Jim Brown House in Boston Township, Summit County, Ohio. Photo courtesy of Tim Fitzwater, Zipper City Photography, Akron, Ohio

Brown and his associates printed notes during a time when no central currency existed in the United States. He manufactured most of his notes from banks in Indiana, although the state was not exclusive for his printing business. He printed notes from local banks and minted bogus coins from many states. Brown's operations spread throughout the Akron area into all of the neighboring counties. It eventually spread all throughout the Midwest.

Besides his printing business, Brown was also involved in stealing horses and other robberies. His crimes were meticulously planned from start to finish. Brown would set up a series of fast horses along his escape route. The animals were placed strategically, so as soon as one horse would tire, another would be available to continue the journey. He could involve himself in a robbery on the opposite side of the state and make it home the following morning. Brown would always make it a point to visit a neighbor. If authorities ever suspected Brown was involved in illegal activity, he would have a well-planned alibi, as the neighbor would vouch that he was home shortly after the robbery would have taken place. This strategy was effective on more than one occasion. Time was always a factor and Brown was able to challenge police on the ability to travel over such long distances in such a short time.

However, neither Jim nor his brother Dan were satisfied operating in the close confines of Akron, Ohio. They dreamed of spreading their operations further out. Their counterfeiting operations were virtually out in the open and they were rarely challenged by the authorities. Both men knew there was money to be made if they could expand their territory, but they could not do it alone. In a time before modern communication and transportation, more manpower was the only option. Here is where Dan Brown became a key figure in the expansion of the gang's operations.

Dan Brown, Jim's brother and a veteran of the War of 1812, was responsible for expanding operations westward along the Ohio River near Indiana. He took large amounts of counterfeit currency and distributed it throughout Ohio, Kentucky, and Indiana. The Brown brothers were assisted by dozens of individuals, but only a few were identified throughout the course of history. Some of the men identified were Colonel William G. Taylor, Colonel William Ashley, Jonathan DeCourcey, Thomas Johnson, Joshua King, Joe Keeler, Abraham

Holmes, George Ulmer, and Perry Randolph. Ashley was from Vermont, doubtfully ever a Colonel, and may possibly be the person who first learned the printing trade. Ashley fled Vermont to an area known as Slab City in Canada, before arriving in the Boston, Ohio area in approximately 1822. DeCourcey was an engraver by trade and likely manufactured the plates. The rest of the men were willing accomplices.

In the early 1830's, Brown sought to permanently expand operations westward. Indiana and Illinois were being settled and Brown realized it was a prime opportunity to establish the organization in those territories. The timing was right, too, as their operations slowly began to catch the eye of local authorities in Summit County.

One of the purposes of this book is to explain how all of the different branches of the organized crime outfit are connected. While you have read this far into the life of James Brown wondering how there is a line between them, it is best explained with Brown's right hand man, a Mr. William Latta. He was born around 1810 in Pennsylvania and moved to Ohio at a young age. At a very young age, Latta married Sarah Sturdivant, in the direct bloodline of Merrick, Roswell, Azar, and James Sturdivant from Cave-in-Rock.

Perry Randolph, George T. Ulmer, and William Latta took the lead on expanding operations to northeast Indiana. The three men had known they were overstaying their welcome in the Akron area and thought it would be a good time to leave. Latta operated a hotel and tavern notorious for harboring thieves and counterfeiters. The hotel Latta operated was located at Ellis' Corners in Copley

31

Township, in the area now known as Montrose, Ohio. Ulmer was a native of Maine but not much is known about his background, or that of Perry Randolph.

Ulmer left for Indiana in 1834. Upon arrival in Indiana, they settled near the border of Lagrange and Noble County in an area called the Tamarack and became one of the first settlers in Noble County. The Tamarack was wet, swampy ground, ideal for criminals who needed a convenient place to hide out. No other group of people would be interested in living in a swamp. Another branch of Brown's organization from nearby Richland County, Ohio, set up shop in Steuben County, Indiana. That band became the Driskel clan, which will be covered shortly.

The group that settled in Steuben County included the families of John Brody and Jon Driskel. Their stop in Steuben did not last long, but Blacklegs reigned in that county for years afterward. They were quickly run out of town by locals who they rubbed the wrong way. The details are sketchy, but it's safe to assume the locals did not take well to strangers setting up a criminal enterprise in their own neighborhood. It is estimated they were only in that region for two to three years before moving further west, settling in Ogle County, Illinois. Their story will be discussed later.

The first person to ever challenge Brown and his criminal enterprise was a man named Samuel Lane, who started out as a newspaper printer and was later elected sheriff of Summit County. Lane began publishing the *Akron Buzzard* in 1837 under the pen name Jedidiah Brownbread to conceal his identity. Lane caused quite a few complications for Brown's gang and those who associated with him. Sheriff Lane openly cautioned the public in the *Akron Buzzard* to stay away

Jim Brown Tavern in Boston Township, Summit County, Ohio. Photo public domain, on file with the National Park Service, Washington D.C.

from Jim Brown and associates, specifically naming Latta as one of the counterfeiters in the area. Lane once penned the question, "Has anyone wondered how it is that Mr. Brown needs such impressive help in the running of a store which stocks under $2,000 in merchandise?" He also warned local residents, "For your own protection, you should note the stature of the men who have taken up storekeeping in the little neighboring town of Boston. They are William G. Taylor of Cleveland; Abraham S. Holmes; Col. William Ashley of Boston; William Latta of Bath; Jonathan DeCourcey and Thomas Johnson of Norton; Joshua King and Joe Keeler of Portage." This was a very dangerous statement for anyone to make at the time.

Eventually Brown and associates figured out who was behind the printing press. Revenge is just business when you are the head of an organized crime syndicate. Lane was assaulted and threatened numerous times. In the middle of the night, Brown's men paid a visit to Lane's business and vandalized the property. Not being fearful of any law enforcement authority, he later sent one of his men to let Lane know who was behind the deed. This serves as testimony to the boldness of Brown and his men.

Sheriff Lane arrested Brown on multiple occasions, but the charges would never stick. Each time Brown would go to jail, he was surrounded by his associates who quickly raised enough money to post his bail. He was always able to get out of the charges one way or another. His trials became more of a source of community entertainment than a means to find justice.

By all accounts, Lane and Brown seemed to have somewhat of a mutual respect for each other. They both understood their roles in life and each tried to outwit the other. One was the criminal and the other was the law enforcer. Brown always seemed to use his high dollar attorneys to ensure his stays in jail did not last long. The 1830's were a prosperous time for Brown's operations. He expanded county by county. Nearly every county history in Ohio tells the tale of counterfeiters infesting their community. There are tales in Lorain County, Cuyahoga County, Warren County, Union County, and down to Hamilton County.

The first sign of real trouble for Brown's gang came in 1834 with the indictment of his associate William Latta. After failing to appear in court, Latta was tracked by the U.S. Marshals from Ohio to the gang's new hideout in Indiana, on a tip provided by none other than James Brown himself. Brown was trying to get himself out of a jam and thought he would turn states evidence.

Latta was taken into custody in 1838 on the charge of possession of counterfeiting equipment and returned to Ohio to face trial. Justice would be delayed, as his trial was postponed until September 1839, giving Latta plenty of time to establish operations far away.

Not surprisingly, Latta once more failed to appear in court and was never heard from again in that area. DeCourcey took the hint, too. After bonding out of jail on his own set of charges, he fled the state, never to be heard from again. There is some evidence that DeCourcey (also spelled Decorsey) moved to Gratiot County, Michigan and gave up his criminal way of life. Regardless, Brown remained determined to keep operations running smoothly, and there were no signs he was deterred by the cases built against DeCourcey and Latta.

The Akron Buzzard, an exposé newspaper printed by former Sheriff Samuel Lane

35

There was one other suspected associate of Brown's who fled around this same time. Julius C. Holliday from the Akron area went east to Butler, Pennsylvania. He began operating a hotel and tavern called the Old Stone House. It soon became a regular stop for those in the crime syndicate who needed a place to stay. It is through the documented history of the Old Stone House that the extent of the syndicate's organization becomes apparent.

Those who knew of the Old Stone House reported visitors using code words to communicate. It was their own unique language, which could only be understood by their associates. This is not the only time the use of code words and secret language was recorded. The men who visited also used fake names and military titles such as "Colonel." This actually suggests there may have been some ranking structure to their operations. No arrests were ever known to be made there, despite the fact the Old Stone House drew the attention of the federal law enforcement authorities.

According to the New Castle News, on October 31, 1931, a local resident recalled federal authorities showing up at one time disguised as a band of musicians, but they were unsuccessful in reigning in any counterfeiters. It was not the law, but rather disease that ended the counterfeiters' control in the Old Stone House. On November 26, 1851, Julius Holliday died of diphtheria. Within weeks, his wife and six children all succumbed to the same disease.

Old Stone House of Butler, Pennsylvania. Used with permission from the Old Stone House Museum, Slippery Rock University

By 1838, Jim and Dan Brown were looking to take their operations to an international level. They considered both Europe and Asia and finally decided on China. The plan was to bring a large amount of counterfeit currency to China to purchase various goods and then return to the United States to sell them. If they could pull it off, this would be a huge money making venture unprecedented at the time. They went with William Taylor and William Ashley down to New Orleans, Louisiana, to put the plan in motion. A large shipping vessel was bought, likely with counterfeit, and the men prepared to leave the following day. Had the plan gone off without a hitch, the history of Brown may have been written differently. However, fate would take Brown in a different direction.

THE

Coin Chart Manual,

SUPPLEMENTARY TO

THOMPSON'S

Bank Note and Commercial Reporter,

CONTAINING FAC SIMILES OF ALL THE

GOLD AND SILVER COINS

FOUND IN CIRCULATION,

THROUGHOUT THE WORLD, WITH THE INTRINSIC VALUE OF EACH.

FORTY-FIRST YEAR OF PUBLICATION.

THOROUGHLY REVISED AND BROUGHT UP TO THE DAY OF GOING TO PRESS.

NEW YORK:

PUBLISHED BY SCOTT & CO.,
146 FULTON STREET.

Thompson's Bank Note and Commercial Reporter, a guide used by bank tellers in the 1800's to determine if coins were real or the work of Jim Brown and associates. (Courtesy of the National Archives, not in copyright)

Before leaving New Orleans for the long voyage to the Far East, the men decided to have one last night out on the town. Their last night turned out to be their downfall, which they would regret forever. Local police became suspicious of Brown and his associates, as they were a bit too lavish with their money. All three men were quickly apprehended on counterfeiting charges and lodged in the local jail. Dan Brown died while he was incarcerated. Taylor, who has been identified as a Lieutenant in the organized crime family, was later acquitted of all charges in New Orleans. Ashley returned to Ohio, where he was convicted on counterfeiting charges and died inside the Ohio Penitentiary in 1838.

Nobody really knows how Brown got out of trouble in New Orleans. There are stories that he testified both for and against Ashley. Either way, he returned to Summit County, where he continued operations stealing horses and passing counterfeit money. As a testament to his abilities as a con artist, he was able to convince the local residents that he was still a respectable citizen even after the incident in New Orleans; so much so that he was elected to the position of Justice of the Peace. He was re-elected on two separate occasions. After relocating to nearby North Hampton in 1845, he became Justice of the Peace there as well. Just like Al Capone, who lived nearly one hundred years later, Brown seemed untouchable by the law. The very man who made a living swindling others was now responsible for bringing justice to the guilty.

Rufus P. Spaulding, former defense attorney for Jim Brown for his trial in the U.S. District Court. Spaulding later was elected to serve Ohio's 18th District in the U.S. House of Representatives.

(Photo courtesy of National Archives, unrestricted use, photo 111-B-1359)

Attorney Noah Swayne, who represented Jim Brown during his trial in U.S. District Court. Swayne was later appointed Justice to the United States Supreme Court by President Abraham Lincoln.

(Photo courtesy of National Archives, unrestricted use, photo 111-B-3277)

Jim Brown's service to the public as Justice of the Peace did not last long, as he was brought up on counterfeiting charges in 1846. His downfall was his greed, from which he had so long profited. Brown decided to counterfeit coins newly issued by the United States. Instead of dealing with the local justice system, which he and his associates had long infiltrated, the case was sent to the United States District Court in Columbus.

In an attempt to get a lighter sentence, Brown turned states evidence on a number of his associates. It did not seem to work too well, as he went before United States Judge John McClean at Columbus in August of that year. Brown was represented by attorneys Rufus Spaulding and Noah Swayne. His assembled defense was an exceptional team. In true gangster style, three of the witnesses who were scheduled to testify against Brown soon found their barns burned to the ground. Although his lawyers were top notch, they were not good enough. The trial resulted in Brown's conviction. After being convicted he was sent to the Ohio Penitentiary in Columbus, where he served a sentence of just less than three years. He was released on July 22, 1849, after serving only two years and eleven months behind bars.

After Brown's release from the Ohio Penitentiary, he went right back into business. By this time operations in Ohio were definitely losing steam. That is not to say his banking operations were going out of business. Brown's associates in Indiana, Illinois, Missouri, and Iowa were running stronger than ever and continued the operation's expansion westward.

Brown's trouble with the law was not over, either. He went up to Michigan, where he was soon arrested on counterfeiting charges and served a short prison sentence. He was eventually released. By all accounts, Brown never stopped involving himself with the crime syndicate until 1865. It wasn't the law that ended Brown's life of crime, either. While jumping from a canal boat, Brown lost his footing and fractured his skull on December 9, 1865. His legacy and life of crime ended when he succumbed to his injuries the following day. He was buried in Boston Cemetery, Summit County, Ohio.

4.   SILE DOTY AND BLACKLEGS

Sometimes referred to as the 'Robin Hood of the Midwest,' Silas "Sile" Doty was an admitted horse thief and counterfeiter who operated mainly in Indiana, Michigan, New York, and Ohio. Although this was home for his operations, he was involved in crime as far east as Massachusetts and as far west as Missouri[1]. Doty was well known regionally during his lifetime, but became famous after a posthumous biography was published about his exploits.

He was a highly respected man in the community, though he spent over half of his life behind bars in Michigan, Indiana, or Ohio. Doty never expressed any remorse to the victims of his crimes. He spent his entire life robbing and stealing, justifying his life as a criminal by often giving away the profits of his crime to the poor. The poor frequently benefited from using counterfeit money in their transactions and by buying stolen property, such as horses, for a fraction of the cost. He was never turned in by his neighbors, as he was rumored to have agreed not to steal from anyone in the surrounding area.

Doty grew up in Bangor, New York, which is in the upper part of the state. As a young boy he had already been accused of stealing, both at a school and at

---

[1] There are allegations that Doty fell in with the Jesse James Gang in Missouri but no factual basis could be found.

home. He fell into the company of William Wicks, who was slightly older than Doty, and they began stealing horses together. In his early twenties, Doty sailed with Wicks across the Atlantic Ocean to England for their first criminal enterprise. They took with them a large amount of goods, which had been stolen from around New York and Canada. While in England, Wicks and Doty stole a number of horses before trying their hand at burglarizing houses. When things heated up too much in England, Wicks and Doty returned to the United States to continue business.

When the 1830's rolled around, Doty traveled with Wicks to the Michigan Territory. Wicks was looking for a fresh start after escaping from jail with a handcuff key crafted by Doty, who was known for his abilities with metal. It was the early days of this region, when Michigan and Ohio were still battling to see which state would own the area of Toledo. Doty stayed in the Detroit area for a short time before heading west to settle in the small town of Adrian, Michigan.

In Michigan, Doty took claim for providing structure and organization to the crime syndicate. It was while he was in Adrian that he met William "Bill" Hill, who introduced him to the area known as the Tamarack, and to the Blacklegs who were organizing operations in northeast Indiana. The extent of the organization Doty provided to the crime syndicate is left up to interpretation, as these claims were all made in his own autobiography. It is difficult to believe all of the accounts that Doty relayed in his own writing, but more difficult to sort out fact from fiction. After all, he lived his entire life taking from others, so honesty was not exactly his best quality. There should be no doubt, though, that Doty's role was one of leadership within the organization.

When things got too hot in Michigan, Doty decided to move again, this time to Indiana. He eventually landed in the Fremont area of Steuben County, Indiana, which was designated Willow Prairie at the time. By the time he arrived in Indiana, he was the well-established leader of criminal activity all throughout the Midwest. Along with the rest of his syndicate, Doty stole horses, robbed travelers, and took anything he could find. His first arrest was around 1839, when he was charged with stealing carpenter's tools from Colonel Alexander Chapin in nearby Orland, Indiana. It was said that Doty agreed not to steal from anyone within twelve miles of his home in Fremont. Orland would have landed right at that twelve-mile mark.

Like any well-versed member of an organized crime outfit, Doty understood there was a code of silence that could not be broken. Unfortunately, Doty's hired farm hand did not understand the unwritten rules of organized crime. In 1839, farm hand Lorenzo Noyes had a falling out with Doty and threatened to go to the authorities, exposing Doty's exploits. Noyes never made it. Doty beat him to death with a hickory stick and concealed the body in a nearby swamp. Doty fled the area before facing justice and found his way to Virginia. After being arrested for theft there, one of Doty's men brought him the necessary tools to escape. He absconded from Virginia and found his way back to the familiar country in northeast Indiana. Doty was still a wanted man, so it was obvious he could not hang his hat at home. He hid out in the Tamarack Swamp, a trading post and haven for Blacklegs to hide out at the time.

It was not until 1842 that Noyes's body was finally found in the nearby

45

swamp. Having already found his way to the Hillsdale County Jail on other charges, the sheriff of Steuben County gave Doty a ride back to the jail in Angola, Indiana. In Angola he was tried and convicted of manslaughter. Doty was given a life sentence in 1844. He was sent to Indiana's first prison in Jeffersonville to serve out the remainder of his life behind bars, or so he may have thought.

It was once said that no jail was strong enough to hold a Blackleg. Doty's jailhouse would soon provide any proof needed. After the Indiana Supreme Court affirmed Doty's motion for a new trial, he was returned to the jail in Angola. Doty was sure that a second trial would end with the same results and his life sentence would be carried out. He cut a hole through the jail floor in Angola, Indiana, and escaped. After escaping from jail he made his way down to the Mexican border. At the time, any individual who enlisted in the military could have their entire background virtually erased and sealed. Although Doty claimed to enlist, it was only another tale in a long list of lies told by the fugitive. He never spent a day of his life in the military and there is no record of him ever serving. Doty bragged that he once stole a horse from then General Zachary Taylor, the same Taylor who would later be elected President of the United States. Doty took advantage of this time in Mexico by stealing and looting anything he could find, peddling the merchandise to American troops fighting the war.

Doty pulled the ultimate scam and convinced his neighbors in Steuben County that he had complete amnesty as a result of his honorable military service. He returned to Steuben County, where nobody ever verified his war stories. There are still some today who believe Doty was a veteran. Doty admits in his biography

MAIL ROBBER. The Buffalo Commercial Advertiser says that Silas Doty has been arrested, charged
with robbing the mail at Fredonia, recently. Several mails and various letters and packages, with at
least $12,000 have been recovered. In the confu-
sion of opening the letters, the robber overlooked
several packages, containing a large amount of
money. The same paper says :

"Doty, the robber, is well known in this city.—
He was formerly a clerk in the post office at Adrian, Michigan. Some months ago he negotiated a
forged draft for $300 upon Mr Randy, the coach-
maker of this city, and was sentenced to serve ten
years in the Michigan penitentiary for the offence,
but through the influence of friends was liberated.
He is represented as a young man of address, writes
an excellent hand, and on leaving Fredonia for this
city in custody of the U. S. Marshal, appended to
his name on the hotel register the initials G. T. T.
—" Gone to Texas."

The Courier, printed December 23, 1841 in Lowell, Massachusetts outlining one of Doty's many crimes (not in copyright)

regarding his military service, "I did not enlist, had no idea of it, but went to robbing, stealing, and killing." He also states, regarding his time in that region, "I had no regular duty with the Army, and for show to business, I engaged as cook for several Officers, which kept me employed during the day." Later, Doty recounts how he returned to New York to visit family and nobody questioned his supposed service. Besides his own admission, there are no military, veteran, or pension records in Doty's name that could be found.

While he did work side by side with various members of the military, Doty himself never served. He would run errands for the General and work odd jobs around the military camps. The only uniform he ever wore was that of the Mexican military, which he used as a costume to conduct robberies of the wealthy locals. Doty not only failed to serve in the military, but he also never served another day in jail for the murder of Noyes. This is not to say Doty never spent any more days in jail at all, however.

Throughout his days in Indiana, Doty continued to visit the Tamarack area to ensure the smooth operation of the crime syndicate. On more than one occasion, he involved himself in the transportation of stolen horses from Indiana back to the Detroit area and other parts of the Midwest. Doty's connections in Michigan went well beyond dropping off a few stolen horses. His associates were involved in one of the era's highest profile criminal cases in Michigan. The case was known as the Railroad Conspiracy case, and it remains one of the largest trials in the state's history. In the court transcripts and records of that trial, the notable name Sile Doty appears numerous times. The extent of Doty or other Blacklegs' involvement in the crimes that lead to the charges in this case are very difficult to determine. Almost every account of the events conflicts with other accounts.

Silas Doty, also went by the name Sile. Reputed head of the Blacklegs criminal organization.

(Photo from the Life of Sile Doty, Blade Printing and Paper Company, not in copyright)

5. SILE DOTY AND ABEL FITCH

In the early 1850's, the State of Michigan was being terrorized by thefts, burglaries, and in some cases, arson. There is a claim that the battle started when the railroads tried to develop land for their enterprise, and as a result would take land away from area farmers. The railroad also refused to reimburse the farmers for livestock killed on the tracks placed through their fields.

Farmers along the railroad routes had previously been reimbursed for any cattle killed by the railroad. They were compensated by the State of Michigan, who owned the railroad and who had the reputation of paying generously for lost livestock. The farmers were understandably upset about not receiving the same level of reimbursement when the railroad companies took over and paid half of what the state had previously paid.

The Railroad Conspirators were involved in a series of attacks and robberies on a railroad in Jackson, Michigan. Eventually, those involved committing arson upon a freight depot in Michigan Centre on April 11, 1851, causing an estimated $150,000 in damage (based upon 1850's figures). Over fifty individuals were arrested and brought to trial in Detroit, Michigan. The trial was highly controversial. One of the lead players the incident, Abel Fitch, was highly respected, though he had had trouble with the law in the past. The first records from Jackson County, Michigan, reflect that he was one of the first men to be placed on trial when the courts were formed, on the charge of conspiracy related to having his hands in the counterfeit business.

History has two stories for Abel Fitch. It is generally agreed that he was a highly regarded state leader, as well as being a key figure in the Underground Railroad. The first story portrays Fitch as a prominent local leader who was framed by men like George Washington Gay, who is largely believed to be responsible for the arson of the depot. Gay was a known associate and friend of Sile Doty.

The other side of the story is that Fitch was the leader of an organized gang who operated in Michigan and openly terrorized the railroad industry. His actions were directly responsible for several deaths attributed to sabotage. The truth likely lies in between these two accounts. There is no doubt that men involved with Fitch were responsible for the arson of the train depot; even their own defense attorney agreed that three or four were responsible. It is also noted that counterfeiting allegations came up throughout the trial against multiple defendants that included Fitch, which is a definite trademark of Blackleg activity.

There are some accounts that Doty met Fitch while he was serving one of his many sentences in Hillsdale County, Michigan. Though Fitch was implicated in the railroad conspiracy, most of the accounts claim that he was not guilty of the accusations made against him in this case. The truth will never be known, as Fitch died in prison on August 25, 1851. How Fitch died remains another mystery. Some accounts say he died of dysentery, while others claim that he took his own life through poisoning.

There are other, more direct, connections to Blacklegs. A man identified as John Hawley of Milford, Indiana, served as a witness in the case. Hawley admitted being at the trading post in Tamarack where McDougall and associates frequented. Hawley was arrested after providing witness testimony for perjury. It was determined he made up his testimony and never met the defendant whom he testified against. Milford (now known as South Milford) is a mere three miles away from the Tamarack, a swamp in Lagrange County, which quickly gained notoriety for being the headquarters of organized crime in the area.

Most of the guilt seems to be pointed at one person, identified as George Washington Gay. This same George Washington Gay once conspired to break Sile Doty out of jail. It is difficult to determine how much of a connection there is between this landmark court case and the associates of Sile Doty. The first reason is that George Washington Gay had a reputation for admitting guilt for crimes in which he was never involved. Because there is so much conflicting information, it is difficult to find the level of actual involvement of the Blacklegs in the Michigan railroad conspiracy. There are a number of connections and coincidences, yet an almost equal number of conflicts. Only the defendants found guilty in the Michigan Railroad Conspiracy case have been added to the list of Blacklegs at the end of this book.

GANG OF COUNTERFEITERS ARREST-
ED!

Deputy U. S. Marshal Mizner, Sherif Bald-
win and City Marshal Warren, accompanied by
a large posse of deputies, returned from Jackson
Co., on Saturday night, having in custody a
gang of thirty malefactors, counterfeiter of U.
S. coin, and other depredators to take their examination before the commissioner.

The notorious Wash. Gay, and a man by the
name of Smith, a hostler, who are supposed to
belong to the same gang, were arrested on Friday, and committed.

Among the persons arrested, were Warner,
of Jackson, Fitch, of Michigan Center, and
others whose names are well known in this
community; and there is little doubt that by
this grand arrest, a formidable gang of evil do-
ers is broken up.

*Report on the arrest of Blacklegs from Michigan. Printed in the
Sandusky Clarion on April 23, 1851 (not in copyright)*

54

History generally confirms that most of the defendants involved in this case were innocent. They were not allowed to take the stand to even present a defense of their own, leaving the record of the actual proceedings questionable. In fact, one report of the events states that the term "railroaded" was a direct result of the public view of the trial.

At the conclusion of the trial in 1851, twelve men were found guilty. Those men were Ammi Filley, a close associate of Abel Fitch, along with Lyman Champlin, Willard Champlin, Erastus Champlin, Richard Price, Ebenzer Price, Orlando Williams, William Corwin, Ebenezer Farhnam, Andrew Freeland, Erastus Smith, and Aaron Mount. All received sentences varying between five and ten years in prison.

The conspirators were transported to the state prison by the same railroad company the men had conspired to destroy. The remaining twenty were cleared of all charges and released. Following the guilty verdicts, several railroad buildings in the Detroit area were soon destroyed by fire. The origin of these fires was never determined. Political strings were later pulled at the highest levels of Michigan government. All those found guilty were released by the Governor of Michigan before their full sentence was served.

The trial itself involved key figures in history. Abel Fitch and the other defendants hired Senator William H. Seward from New York to provide their defense. More notably, Seward would become Secretary of State for Abraham Lincoln. An assassination attempt was made on Seward the same night Lincoln's life was taken. Seward would later be involved in the 1867 deal, which resulted in the purchase of land now known as Alaska. The Prosecutor in the case, James VanDyke, would later be elected Mayor of the City of Detroit.

Some historical accounts portray all the defendants as respectable men who were framed by greedy corporate executives who sought to expand their railroad. This is far from the truth. Almost all of the men convicted in this case had previous records. Orlando D. Williams had at least one previous arrest for counterfeiting, as did another defendant named Ebenezer Farnham. Defendant William Corwin had a more violent history of assault charges and one for larceny. Andrew Freeland had known ties to the Blacklegs and had a previous conviction for assaulting his own father. Defendant Erastus Champlin had previously served prison time in New York, and his sons were following the same path. Finally, defendant Aaron Mount had previous counterfeiting charges in New York and larceny charges in both Jackson and Washtenaw counties in Michigan.

As in other cases, Blacklegs were able to secure pardons through their political connections. Even in this case, the men involved would later receive pardons from Governor McClelland, Governor Parsons, and later Governor Bingham, even though some openly admitted responsibility for certain aspects of the crime. Three of the men agreed not to renew their attacks on the railroad property if they were granted a pardon. So the fact that these twelve men would later receive pardons is irrelevant to their names being added to the list of identified Blacklegs. Their involvement in the crime is also evidenced by their efforts to confirm a pardon.

Although Doty was never charged in the Railroad Conspiracy case, he did have a court case of his own at the same time. In 1851, over two dozen of his associates were arrested in the Hillsdale area for stealing horses and passing counterfeit. Most of his associates earned seven years in the penitentiary. Doty was sentenced to seventeen years in prison, but was let out early as a reward for good behavior.

SERVED HIS TIME.—The Jackson *Citizen* of Wednesdany last, states that the notorious Silas Doty, of Hillsdale county, was discharged from the State prison on Monday morning, having served out his second term in that institution, which was upwards of 17 years, or till he arrived at the age of three score and ten. Doty's exploits at theift—or what he termed business transactions; in this and adjoining counties, have not been forgotten by those whom he dealt with.

October 23, 1866 edition of the Hillsdale Standard, Hillsdale, Michigan (not in copyright)

Doty wasn't out long before he stole a horse in Coldwater, Michigan and found his way down to Bryan, Ohio. He was arrested there, as he couldn't outrun the telegraph, which had notified area authorities that he was on the run once again. Doty would spend the next four years behind bars once more in Jackson, Michigan, at the state penitentiary.

Despite all of his criminal exploits, it is important to know that Doty remained a respected man of the community. He did provide some level of community service, as he was known to regularly give his stolen proceeds to needy neighbors. If a neighbor needed farm equipment, tools, or other implements, one word to Doty would make their requests manifest in no time at all. It was a situation where nobody asked questions, as they feared the answers. How much of Doty's respect was earned from fear may never be known. For whatever reason, society does lend a certain respect to organized crime figures, just as they did with John Gotti, Al Capone, and other more recently recognized figures. Doty was equally respected a century earlier.

Doty stopped stealing only when he took his last breath. In March of 1876, Doty took that last breath the day after his own horse was reportedly stolen. He died in Reading, Michigan, never once expressing remorse for his victims. Doty is buried in Kinderhook, Michigan, near his former home town of Fremont, Indiana. His legacy of fraud continues to this day, as he is still recognized as a veteran of the Mexican-American War.

Gravesite of Silas Doty, identified only by his initials. Still recognized as a military veteran today. Photo used with permission from the collection of Christine Pellor of Carmel, Indiana

6. THE TOWNSEND GANG

Besides Doty's link to the Tamarack, he does have one other tie to the organized crime syndicate. That connection is through Bill Hill, the man who originally introduced Doty to the syndicate in northeast Indiana. Bill Hill's story may be just as interesting as Doty's, though less is known about him. A link can also be found in obscure references in the reporting of Doty's associate Gregor McDougall, which mentioned he was part of the "Townsend Gang." The case will be made that William "Bill" Hill was none other than William Townsend, the same notorious William Townsend who lead a vicious gang in Canada, and who was the head of the "Townsend Gang" which covered New York and Upper Canada. These areas quickly became known for robberies and counterfeiting, and eventually a brutal murder.

William Townsend was born in the former city of Black Rock, New York, which is now nothing more than the name of a neighborhood in Buffalo. Townsend came from a good family whose roots can be traced back to Sir Robert Townsend of Plymouth in 1530. His father, Robert Townsend, was a well-respected carpenter in the area where Townsend spent his childhood.

There is no real documentation as to when Townsend first began his life of crime. He was known to have worked on various ships throughout the 1840's. It is possible he was involved in crime back then, but certainly after 1850 his occupation had changed. Almost every reference after 1850 refers to him as "the notorious Townsend." Townsend's notoriety was due to the sheer number of crimes he was involved in, as well as the manner in which he carried himself. One of Townsend's notable qualities was that of being a very good actor. This quality is key in establishing the likelihood that Townsend and Hill were more than likely the same person.

Sketch of the person believed to be William Townsend, on trial in Canada (not in copyright)

Although one of Townsend's accomplices stated that he once bragged of killing six men, there is no substantial evidence of bloodshed until October 18, 1854. After committing several robberies earlier that day, Townsend went with his accomplices George King, John Blowes, William Bryson, John Lettice, and another man by the name of Weaver to the home of John Hamilton Nelles,[2] who was known to be a wealthy individual. Nelles lived with his family near Cayuga, Ontario, in an area now known as Nelles Corners. After entering his home, Townsend and his gang immediately shot Nelles. Nelles collapsed with a fatal wound. He was robbed of his money and a gold watch, and later died of his wounds.

A manhunt immediately ensued to catch those responsible. One by one, Townsend's associates King, Bryson, and Blowes were taken into custody and were placed on trial near Cayuga. All three were convicted and anxiously awaited sentencing before the court. Bryson was the first of the three allowed to address the court and make his last statement before the judge. Suspecting he would be put to death, Bryson proclaimed his innocence on the charge of murder. Before Bryson could finish his statement, King interrupted with his own declaration of innocence. Blowes only smiled nefariously, remained silent, and said nothing, as if the death sentence were a welcome friend.

All three men stood before the judge to await his decision. As suspected, the penalty given was death by hanging. Bryson and King immediately broke down in

---

2 There was one other man named Patterson linked with the Nelles Murder. It was later determined Patterson was not present and he was never charged.

tears. Blowes was coldly indifferent to being informed his life would end that same month. A sympathetic judge later commuted Bryson's sentence to life in prison, but King and Blowes were not as lucky. They were hanged by the neck for the murder of Nelles on May 18, 1855.

There are two stories regarding Lettice. The first report states that he was shot and killed on the ice by police while making his escape to the United States. The second take is that he was shot and killed during a botched burglary in New York later that year. Weaver was the easiest to catch, as he died of tuberculosis long before the police could find him.

Townsend was a master criminal and was successful in his escape. During Townsend's departure, he shot up to four officers who were attempting to take him into custody. One of the men, Constable Charles Richards, came the closest to capturing the notorious Townsend. Richards caught Townsend red handed in the middle of one of his many burglaries. Townsend gave the lawman one firm warning. He then carefully pulled out his revolver, hastily pointed it toward the Constable, and squeezed the trigger. Richards would only live another four hours before succumbing to his wounds.

Townsend is believed to have first gone back to his hometown near Buffalo to hide out. He stayed with family, hoping he could evade capture. His niece later claimed that the clever Townsend would hide in plain sight by wearing women's clothing. Others who knew Townsend confirmed this story and said he would dress up as his twin sister just for show, and was very good at it. When things heated up in the Buffalo area, he went on the run throughout Canada before eventually heading for Ohio.

After arriving in Cleveland, coincidentally close to the area of James Brown's gang, Townsend decided to grab a drink at the New London Porter House. Unfortunately for him, the saloon happened to be owned and operated by a Canadian named John Iles. Iles was a hotel keeper in Cleveland and had known Townsend as someone who would regularly patronize the bars in the City of London, Ontario. Iles was also aware that Townsend was wanted for the murder of Nelles. After dropping a glass in the shock of having Townsend walk into his bar, Iles contacted the police, who quickly apprehended the fugitive before anyone else was hurt. When he was searched by Constable McCarthy, Townsend was found to be in possession of three knives and fourteen cents in change.

The difference between the Townsend case and the case later made against McDougall is that there was no doubt about Townsend's guilt. Everyone agreed that Townsend and his men had murdered Nelles and Richards. When Townsend was finally extradited and put on trial for murder, the case had little to do with proving his guilt. Rather, it sought to conclude whether or not the man who was taken into custody in Cleveland was actually Townsend.

It was a long, drawn out, controversial, and well documented trial. The trial included over one hundred witnesses who testified that the man both was and was not the notorious Townsend. Twice as many witnesses testified that the man was in fact Townsend. Friends and family gave conflicting testimony, causing significant confusion amongst the jurors. This was long before the advent of fingerprints, photographs, or any other identification techniques used by police today. In September 1857, a few months before McDougall was hanged, the Townsend case came back with a hung jury and the defendant was released. The trial cost the Canadian government an estimated $40,000. The cost of this trial was unheard of for the day.

At the completion of the first trial, the jury did not find enough evidence to affirm the defendant was in fact Robert Townsend. After the jury freed the defendant, he was immediately arrested again on robbery charges. Those charges were from a robbery committed by Townsend so the police felt they still had enough evidence they had their man. If the man on trial actually was Townsend, he was a good enough actor to raise doubt amongst the jury. He was never brought to trial again. It is still unknown if the man was actually Townsend, as he disappeared and was never seen again.

7.   WILLIAM "BILL" HILL

Who was the man known as William "Bill" Hill? This is a difficult question to answer, as there is a complete lack of documentation for the man known as Hill. There is no documentation that discusses his family history, early years, or any other biographical information. This is unusual, as the rest of the crime family can be positively traced. The first mention of him is through the biography of Sile Doty, when they became acquainted in Michigan. Everything else known about the man known as Hill can be found in documentation of the Blacklegs in Indiana.

There are several important factors which suggest that the man known in Noble County as William Hill was actually the notorious Townsend in hiding under this alias name. Several books from that era reference the fact that William Hill went by the nickname of Townsend. Hill was reportedly absent from Noble County during the time the individual thought to be Townsend was captured in Cleveland, Ohio and brought to Canada. A time line of the documented events in the lives of both Hill and Townsend show the two were never in the same place at the same time. Descriptions of both men certainly reveal that their less than sunny dispositions and were virtually identical. Both were described as cold, hardened criminals. The same book reported that friends of the man known as Bill Hill later found him in Missouri, alive and well, living the life of a farmer.

The first person to suggest Hill and Townsend may be one and the same was

Robert Waddell, when he wrote his <u>History of Northeast Indiana</u>. Waddell wrote of Hill, "He it was who organized at Cayuga Fairs, Canada, a band of young men, who robbed many stores, stole horses, and committed one murder. The band was at last dispersed by Dominion officials. Two were hanged, one was shot on the ice in a field near Windsor in an effort to reach the state line." In 1856-57, while Hill was absent on one of his trips to unknown parts, a man was arrested in Kent County, Canada, where McDougall came from, who was thought to be Townsend. The court was unable to prove his identity, though it was testified to by a young man of his gang, who had been arrested and who was sent to prison for life. It is a thorough reflection of the activities of Townsend, giving credit to the man known as William Hill. This connection between Hill and Townsend faded over the course of time, but now seems more important than ever.

The man known as Hill certainly had some well-documented exploits with the Blacklegs of Indiana. Outside of the references in McDougall's background, which mention that he was recruited by Townsend, there is no evidence that Townsend ever visited Indiana. This is unusual, as it was a known haven for outlaws to hide out. A man on the run from Canada for murder who was a known accomplice of the gang would have certainly found refuge in the swamps of Indiana. Unless, of course, he was hiding out there under the assumed name of Hill. The final piece of evidence that supports the idea that Hill and Townsend were the same man can be found later when the aftermath of McDougall's execution is discussed.

There is one other interesting connection involving William Townsend. While he was on the run, one of the rumors circulating was that he was working as a performer in a Minstrel Troupe. He was a performer for the Van Amburgh & Co.'s Circus, which operated from 1845 until 1881. It was said that Townsend was recognized while performing for the circus near Rock Island, Illinois, the city where Colonel Davenport was murdered by members of the Driskel-Brody gang. As Townsend reportedly had the skills of a good actor, this story may have merit.

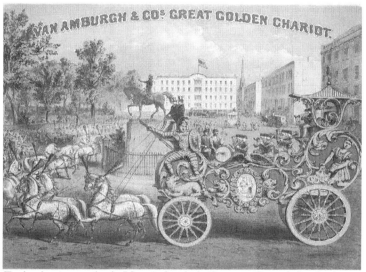

Early advertisement for the Van Amburgh & Company Circus, believed to be used as a hideout for Townsend (not in copyright)

8. THE DRISKEL GANG

Although the Driskel[3] Gang has been connected to Sile Doty in the past, it is likely the men were originally associates of Jim Brown. The Driskel family originated in Ohio a short distance from Jim Brown in Summit County. Members of the Driskel Gang left Ohio at a very troubling time for Brown's gang, when things began to heat up in the court system for those involved in the crime syndicate. It is much more likely they began their criminal operations under the command of Brown than Doty, expanding the organization's operations westward at the direction of Brown.

Although he had eight other children, John Driskel was only known to be involved in his criminal enterprises with his sons Taylor, Pierce, David, and William. They were some of the earliest identified outlaws in Ohio. They first settled in Wayne County in the early 1800's, right around the time Ohio gained statehood. John Driskel had previously lived in Columbiana County, where there were rumors that he had difficulties getting along with others. John began his criminal lifestyle long before Jim Brown settled in Summit County, but there is no evidence of their involvement in any organized crime until later. It was also through the Driskel Gang that the first mention of a vigilante group appears to have been organized. Known as the 'Black Cane Society' for the color of the canes they carried to signify their membership, the society was known to have made a

---

[3]   The last name was recorded various ways to include Driscoll, Driskill, and Driskel.

number of arrests in an early, unsuccessful effort to quash the activities of Blacklegs in Ohio. Though it is not documented, the society may have been the reason why the Driskel family chose to relocate, as they had a habit of doing multiple times.

In their days in Wayne County, the Driskels lived in an area called Stibbs Mill. Genealogical records from the family of William Latta, one of the chief players for Jim Brown, say that the Latta's were once regular visitors to Stibbs Mill, an area near Wooster, Ohio. Stibbs Mill was a good hideout for anyone involved in criminal activity. It was in a remote location at the time, used as a mill and small store where the Indians and other locals were known to buy and sell goods. The Driskel gang was not in Wayne County very long before getting into some serious trouble. John Driskel was arrested on a minor theft charge after being accused of stealing a candlestick from a local bar.

The candlestick theft seems relatively trivial compared to Driskel's other exploits. Driskel would soon find himself serving his first term in the Ohio Penitentiary after he stole a few horses in Columbiana County, Ohio. He was found in Pennsylvania and extradited back to Ohio where he was placed on trial. Driskel, described as being "strong as an ox but much meaner," escaped from a chain gang and worked his way back to Wayne County. He was recaptured and sent back to the penitentiary, but never made it there.

Driskel escaped custody on his way to prison. He realized that pushing his luck would only place him back behind bars, so he fled Ohio and settled in Steuben County, Indiana. His friend Steven Brody and family, who found themselves in their own mess with the law in Ohio, would soon arrive to keep him company. The Driskel-Brody clan first moved to Steubenville, a small village in the southern portion of Steuben County, east of the current town of Ashley. Historical accounts state the Driskel-Brody gang only stayed two or three years in Steuben County (home of Sile Doty) before they wore out their welcome. As they did many times, the gang relocated west to expand criminal operations.

Driskel, Brody, and their associates arrived in Ogle County, Illinois, in approximately 1835 or 1836.[4] Their crime of choice was the same: counterfeiting and stealing horses. Kett noted in his *History of Ogle County, Illinois*, that Driskel settled in an area he named Killbuck Creek, after an area where he had previously lived in Ohio. The Killbuck Creek in Ohio is located near Mansfield, which would be south of Jim Brown's hometown in Summit County. This is one of the only clues that gives us insight on the trail of Driskel and Brody.

The Driskels operated mainly in Ogle County, but their syndicate plagued nearby Winnebago, Dekalb, McHenry, Boone, and Lee Counties. Perhaps the best way to relay the extent of operations is to use the actual description from the History of Winnebago County: "Extending from Wisconsin down through Illinois into Missouri and Arkansas, there was unquestionably a line of horse thieves, along which stolen horses were almost continuously passing. The line had convenient stations, and the stations were in charge of men, who, to all outward appearances were honest, hard-working settlers. Under this arrangement a horse stolen at either

---

4   The Illinois State Legislature recognized Brody as settling the area in 1836 in a resolution recognizing the 150th Anniversary of the establishment of the Village of Creston (though no mention Brody was an outlaw).

end of the line, or anywhere in its vicinity in the interior, for that matter, could be passed from one agent to another and no one of the agents be absent from his home or business for more than a few hours at a time." What advantage would a person have for secreting stolen horses? For one, their house and property would not be targeted for robberies. The other advantage would be financial gain. The Blacklegs had "adjusters" who would travel along the routes of the horse thieves. They would provide a payoff to each member who would assist the syndicate through various means. How would you possibly stand a chance of fighting a criminal element as organized and extensive as the Blacklegs?

The residents of Ogle County, however, soon began to fight back. They quickly grew weary of their horses being stolen and their merchants being inundated with counterfeit money. Author H. Kett's description in the History of Ogle County, Illinois is almost identical to what can be found in the local histories of Noble and Lagrange counties from that same era. He writes, "Up to 1841 no decisive measures had been inaugurated to rid the country of the presence of the villains that had apparent control of everything. The laws could not be enforced with any degree of efficiency. If arrested, tried and found sufficiently guilty to hold them to a bail, there were no jails sufficiently secure to hold them; and even if there had been, there were members of the gang abundantly able to offer any amount of bail required. Witnesses were always present to prove an alibi, and thus it came about that the ranks of the prairie pirates were never thinned by law processes." It was a true sign of the extent of the organized crime problem that existed at the time.

Similar to the situation that would begin to occur in Noble County, Indiana, the gang had infiltrated the criminal justice system with men on their own payroll. The judge and sheriff were both well known to be associates of the Driskel-Brody clan. At the same time Driskel and Brody were in their prime, the first efforts to rid northeast Indiana of the same type of organized crime occurred at Stone's Tavern. Unfortunately, efforts in both Indiana and Illinois proved futile against the strong reaches of organized crime.

In April 1841, a group of men met at White Rock, Illinois in a log school house, likely built by the syndicate themselves, who were some of the first settlers in the area. They realized the criminal justice system was ineffective and inefficient, so they organized themselves as vigilantes. They would deal with horse thieves by stripping and violently lashing them until compliance was gained. They would rid their region of organized crime and pledged they would sacrifice their lives if necessary as part of this effort.

Just as the first efforts at Stone's Tavern failed, so did the initial efforts in Ogle County. After several members of the outfit were arrested and housed in the Ogle County Jail on counterfeiting charges, their associates came to their aid. The courthouse caught on fire the same night the first arrests were made and was burned to the ground. Although the court records were safe at the home of the local clerk, the jury was not safe from the poisonous corruption that plagued the area. A tainted jury allowed the accused to go free, infuriating the local residents who were understandably growing tired of being crime victims.

The citizens formed their own version of the Black Cane Society that had been established in Ohio. They formed themselves into companies of volunteer citizen law enforcers, calling themselves "Regulators." Their purpose lay in the detection of horse thieves, counterfeiters, and other criminals. The biggest difference was how the Regulators were authorized in Indiana versus the way they were first formed in Illinois. While the Regulators in Indiana were formed pursuant to a new law passed in Indiana, the Illinois Regulators were formed at the suggestion of a local judge and did not have the backing of any legislation.

The Regulators knew exactly what was going on, what they were doing, and who was responsible. As described in the History of Dekalb County: "Into this the horses were taken and secured during the day and at night were removed to stations further north, as the horse thieves found an excellent market for their stolen property in the lumber districts of Wisconsin. The line of travel was usually from Brodie's Grove to Gleason's at Genoa, Henpeck now Old Hampshire in Kane County, thence north through McHenry County into Wisconsin." It didn't take long before the Regulators began to take action.

The Regulators had a different take on how to deal with the local criminals who terrorized their community. According to Kett, they first tried corporal punishment. Blacklegs in the area were taken into custody by Regulators. The first individual arrested was stripped and given thirty-six lashes. The man identified as John Hurl[5] followed the identical path of a man named Miles Payne, who will be discussed later. Rather than face further punishment, Hurl joined up in the company of Regulators to rid the area of the criminal element. Hurl would have

---

[5]   Hurl's name was also recorded as Harl.

been in a unique situation, being considered a traitor to his former conspirators and looked at with some level of distrust by the Regulators.

The Regulators of Ogle County obtained their confessions by means similar to their counterparts in Indiana: with all force available to them at the time. Instead of pulling their suspects off the ground by a rope tied around their neck, the Regulators of Illinois used the method of strapping their suspects to a tree and giving them lashes to encourage reluctant cooperation. The method also proved to be an effective means in identifying others involved in their criminal organization. Some of those found guilty were run out of town with promises they would never return. Undoubtedly, this method produced the names of Driskel and Brody as being the chief operators of the crime syndicate.

Driskel's Gang, also known as the Prairie Pirates, were much more confrontational with the Regulators who sought to take control over the criminal organization. When the first leader of the Regulators was identified, the Driskel-Brody gang immediately sent a message to intimidate. They broke the legs of a horse owned by Regulator Captain W.S. Wellington and left the animal for dead. The intimidation efforts worked, as Wellington immediately resigned and ceased his activities with the Regulators.

The reins were soon picked up by a new Regulator Chief named John Campbell. Kett reported that William Driskel once sent a letter filled with threats to kill Campbell. The letter did not work, and Campbell remained more determined than ever. After a series of confrontations between the Driskel Gang and Regulators, it appears these Prairie Pirates followed through on their word.

David and Taylor Driskel lay in wait in Campbell's yard on June 27, 1841. When Campbell went toward the gate to his house, the Driskels asked him for directions. David Driskel squeezed the trigger of his rifle, shooting Campbell in the chest. Campbell fell back and died on the spot.

Ogle County was now a powder keg with a lit fuse. The Regulators were more determined than ever to punish the Prairie Pirates, with or without the assistance of law enforcement. From reading various accounts of intervention attempts made by the local sheriff and other representatives of the criminal justice system, it appears that these representatives were just as much a part of the problem. The sheriff would later be brought up on his own set of charges related to being a Driskel Gang sympathizer, and for failing to fulfill the duties of the

Regulator Phineas Chaney of Ogle County, once targeted for assassination by the Driskel Gang. He was first on the scene when John Campbell was murdered (not in copyright)

office. As no impartial justice system could be found, the Regulators of Ogle

County decided to take the law into their own hands and create one. Although he was not the trigger man, the sheriff had arrested John Driskel and placed him into custody in the local jail. His two sons, William and Pierce Driskel, were also quickly apprehended at their homes in Dekalb County, Illinois by a band of Regulators. Other members of the gang, which included David Driskel, Thomas Aikens, Richard Aikens, and Taylor Driskel, escaped from the Regulator excitement. While this band of organized criminals was known for breaking out of jail, this time it was the Regulators involved in the jail break. Not trusting that the local system would bring justice to the men who murdered Campbell, the Regulators arrived at the Ogle County Jail to ensure that action would be taken. The sheriff, a known associate of the gang, was outnumbered. John Driskel and his sons were hastily turned over to the custody of local Regulators, who planned their own trial. A local resident named Edwin S. Leland was appointed to the role of judge to hear the case made against Driskel. The trial would be before a jury, but not the average one. The jury was comprised of one hundred and twenty local citizens (some of them noted as being slightly intoxicated). The jury would avenge the death of Campbell with frontier style justice.

After the best trial the local citizens could offer, Pierce was released solely on the basis of his age as he was the youngest, and perhaps a bit of sympathy for what was coming next. John Driskel and his son William did not fare so well. The first decision was to hang Driskel, but his last request was to be shot. The Regulators of Ogle County happily obliged. John and William[6] were both taken

---

[6] Some accounts indicate William Driskel admitted to six murders, however there are no

before a group of just over one hundred men armed with rifles and ordered to their knees. Both men were placed in a hole. Less than a dozen men had live ammunition so that the true executors could not be identified. The signal was given and the triggers were pulled. The men were executed by the quasi (but effective) firing squad on June 29, 1841. The dirt from the hole where they executed was heaped over their bodies. Justice had been served with or without the criminal justice system which had failed the citizens of Ogle County, just as it would soon fail those in northeast Indiana.

The execution of the Driskels did not go without some attempt at punishment by the established justice system. All of the Regulators who were present for the execution of John and William were indicted on murder charges for their participation, even though they didn't know who was actually responsible. The indicted men wisely asked for a jury trial. The jury was undoubtedly stacked full of local residents who had lived through the terror caused by Driskel and his associates. By all accounts, the trial seemed to be more of a formality to clear the Regulators of any wrongdoing, as opposed to an actual trial to find justice. The system which had worked against law-abiding citizens for so long was now in the hands of those very same citizens. Most of the time taken up by the trial was reading off the names of those accused, a lengthy list of every man who had a gun the day of the execution. The Prosecutor called a minimal number of witnesses, none of whom could provide any direct evidence against the accused.

_____

victims' names recorded to verify the allegations.

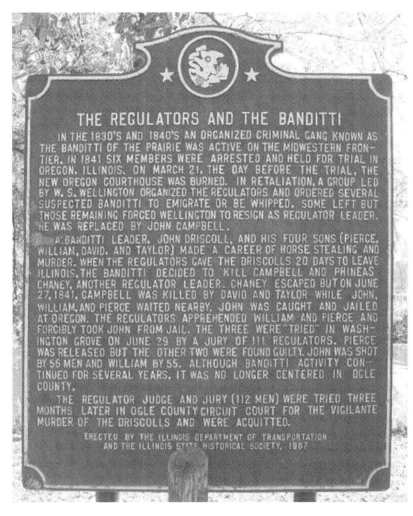

THE REGULATORS AND THE BANDITTI

IN THE 1830'S AND 1840'S AN ORGANIZED CRIMINAL GANG KNOWN AS THE BANDITTI OF THE PRAIRIE WAS ACTIVE ON THE MIDWESTERN FRONTIER. IN 1841 SIX MEMBERS WERE ARRESTED AND HELD FOR TRIAL IN OREGON, ILLINOIS. ON MARCH 21, THE DAY BEFORE THE TRIAL, THE NEW OREGON COURTHOUSE WAS BURNED. IN RETALIATION, A GROUP LED BY W. S. WELLINGTON ORGANIZED THE REGULATORS AND ORDERED SEVERAL SUSPECTED BANDITTI TO EMIGRATE OR BE WHIPPED. SOME LEFT BUT THOSE REMAINING FORCED WELLINGTON TO RESIGN AS REGULATOR LEADER. HE WAS REPLACED BY JOHN CAMPBELL.

A BANDITTI LEADER, JOHN DRISCOLL, AND HIS FOUR SONS (PIERCE, WILLIAM, DAVID, AND TAYLOR) MADE A CAREER OF HORSE STEALING AND MURDER. WHEN THE REGULATORS GAVE THE DRISCOLLS 20 DAYS TO LEAVE ILLINOIS, THE BANDITTI DECIDED TO KILL CAMPBELL AND PHINEAS CHANEY, ANOTHER REGULATOR LEADER. CHANEY ESCAPED BUT ON JUNE 27, 1841, CAMPBELL WAS KILLED BY DAVID AND TAYLOR WHILE JOHN, WILLIAM, AND PIERCE WAITED NEARBY. JOHN WAS CAUGHT AND JAILED AT OREGON. THE REGULATORS APPREHENDED WILLIAM AND PIERCE AND FORCIBLY TOOK JOHN FROM JAIL. THE THREE WERE "TRIED" IN WASHINGTON GROVE ON JUNE 29 BY A JURY OF 111 REGULATORS. PIERCE WAS RELEASED BUT THE OTHER TWO WERE FOUND GUILTY. JOHN WAS SHOT BY 56 MEN AND WILLIAM BY 55. ALTHOUGH BANDITTI ACTIVITY CONTINUED FOR SEVERAL YEARS, IT WAS NO LONGER CENTERED IN OGLE COUNTY.

THE REGULATOR JUDGE AND JURY (112 MEN) WERE TRIED THREE MONTHS LATER IN OGLE COUNTY CIRCUIT COURT FOR THE VIGILANTE MURDER OF THE DRISCOLLS AND WERE ACQUITTED.

ERECTED BY THE ILLINOIS DEPARTMENT OF TRANSPORTATION AND THE ILLINOIS STATE HISTORICAL SOCIETY, 1967

Historical Marker: The Regulators and the Banditti, located six miles north of Oregon, Illinois. Photo courtesy of Ben Schoepski from the collection at www.schoepski.com

Without even leaving the courtroom for deliberations, the jury returned a "not guilty" verdict against all of the Regulators who had been indicated. They apparently already had their decision without a need to talk amongst each other. All of the men were acquitted of all charges and returned to a more peaceful Ogle County.

The story of the Driskel Gang, how they were dispatched by Regulators, and the after-effect of their actions undoubtedly reached the stretches of Noble and Lagrange County. Perhaps the formation of Regulator Companies in the then-rural counties influenced the State legislature of Indiana to authorize the formation of similar associations. The way in which justice was brought to the Driskel gang may have also been influential in later years, when the Regulators of Indiana were contemplating ways to deal with their own den of thieves. After witnessing the criminal justice system fail, they may have known that there was only one guaranteed way justice could be found. For the Regulators of Indiana, their attempt to establish law and order was made in the judgment of a young man named Gregor McDougall around the very same time.

It was determined, after John and William were already executed, that David Driskel was the actual trigger man. A $500 reward was offered for the arrest of David and Taylor. David Driskel was later shot and killed by a sheriff in nearby Iowa. Taylor Driskel turned himself in to authorities years later and was placed on trial by an established court for the murder of John Campbell. He was acquitted of murder, mostly due to the lack of witnesses or evidence.

Most of Driskel's accomplices also fled the area. Norton B. Royce was one of those men. Royce was born in Delaware County, Ohio, and moved with Driskel to Ogle County, Illinois. Once the Driskel gang was broken down by the Regulators, Royce fled to Missouri. In February 1847, Royce escaped from the jail in St. Louis by removing a stone out of the third story and lowering himself to the ground with torn bed sheets. By 1851, Royce made is way to Wisconsin and began farming. He later settled in Rich Hill, Missouri. There is no evidence Royce continued Blackleg activity after the lynching of the Driskels. Pierce Driskel moved to Chicago, and by all accounts led the normal, crime-free life of a farmer in nearby Dekalb County, Illinois.

Organized crime in the area continued long after the execution of the Driskels. Things did not appear to slow down in this region of Illinois until 1845. The majority of blacklegs decided it was time to live a more peaceful life, and they identified all of their fellow conspirators to the Regulators. Two of the blacklegs captured included William McDowell and Charles Oliver Jr., suspected of being some of the leaders. Most of the remaining Blacklegs were beaten and ordered never to return.

Oliver was held without bail until his trial began on August 26, 1845. He was charged with the robbery of William Mulford of Guilford, Illinois. Oliver and his gang heard rumors that the Mulford's had $15,000 in their house. If they did in fact have that amount of money, Oliver was unsuccessful at extracting the cash during the robbery. They took whatever money the Mulfords did have and ran. Their flight was short-lived, as the increasing number of Regulators made their escape much more difficult. During the trial, Oliver's associate Irving Stearns testified that Oliver bought a horse with part of the stolen money. Another associate named West testified to receiving some stolen money but denied participating in the robbery. The "bold and defiant" Oliver was convicted, but his life was spared. He was sent to the state penitentiary to serve eight years. After five years he received a pardon and moved back to New York with his wife and family.

McDowell would share a similar fate as Oliver. He was convicted and sentenced to serve eight years in the state penitentiary at Alton, Illinois. McDowell too received a pardon after only five years. He also stopped his association with the Blacklegs and appears to have lived the remainder of his life peacefully and crime free in that same region of Illinois.

History shows that the Regulators offered little apology for not executing those actually involved in the murder, but they were subject to open criticism at the time. This History of Winnebago County confirms this by reporting from a local publication: "No one pretends that John and William Driskel had not committed murder, nor can they say that they merited the punishment they received, even had they been found guilty by an impartial jury of their country of the crime alleged by the mob." Through they received criticism, the general population was more interested in ridding their community of the syndicate.

Historical marker at the site of the Driscoll execution in Illinois

9.   BLACKLEGS CONTINUANCE

Similar to how the Driskels moved west, there was another small band of Blacklegs that began in Indiana and then moved westward. This smaller group first made their home in both Clay and Owen Counties in southwestern Indiana. The families involved in this regional Blackleg activity were the Phipps and Long families.

The Phipps family consisted of Jesse and William Phipps, who moved to the area from North Carolina. Jesse Phipps was rumored to be the leader of the southwestern Indiana Blacklegs and passed the family trade along to his sons, John Meshack and Eli Shadrack Phipps. These two men were twin brothers, and coincidentally are the longest living set of twins in history. The Long family consisted of Owen Long and his sons, John and Aaron.

Just as the Blacklegs did elsewhere, anyone arrested in this area did not stay in jail long. They would either bond out, get assistance from insiders in the court system, or they would be broken out of jail by their companions. That is not to say there were never any attempts to find justice through the courts, however.

The first time John Long went on trial was in Clark County, Indiana. By the time Long was arrested, the jail was already full of horse thieves - as many as the small log cabin jail could hold. When Long was brought before the Judge, his attorney argued that the horse was of no value; that the horse was actually a gelding. The argument failed and Long was sentenced to receive thirty-nine lashes. Before the sentence was executed, Long's attorney tried arguing that there was no proof the horse had been stolen in Indiana. The Judge appeased Long's attorney until the court was adjourned. As the local residents filed out of the courtroom, the Judge calmly ordered the Sheriff to take Long out into the woods and give him thirty-nine lashes on his bare back, and to have him in court the following day. The Sheriff was ordered to keep the sentence secret and not talk about it. The following day, the Judge agreed to give Long a new trial. The whipping must have brought some sense to Long, as he jumped up and had his attorney withdraw the motion to avoid receiving another similar punishment.

Just as would be seen later in northern Indiana, the citizens formed themselves into Regulator companies to take justice into their own hands. Long was not the only one to receive a whipping as punishment for stealing horses. In one documented case, one of his fellow conspirators, John Phipps, was tied up to a tree and whipped when justice could not be found through the established courts.

The Blackleg activity in Clay and Owen Counties did not last long. Either through whippings, lynchings, or other violence directed toward this band of thieves, they soon knew their welcome was worn out. Though members of the Phipps and Long families remained in the area, they seemed to commit most of

John Meshack Phipps (1812-1916), one of the few photographs of any Blacklegs that exist. Phipps and his brother hold the record for the longest living twins. (not in copyright)

their criminal activity in neighboring Illinois. There were documented incidents involving Blacklegs from as early as the 1820's and leading through the 1830's in Illinois. These incidents occurred in Morgan and Scott Counties. It would eventually include Hancock County, which experienced the first violence between anti-Mormons. The activity was widespread throughout the pioneer days of Illinois and it was just as organized as ever. There were documented Regulator efforts to wash out this organized band of thieves in at least sixteen counties throughout Illinois, and just as many in Iowa. Though the Driskels were not around to call the shots anymore, it does not appear that the syndicate suffered from any shortage of leadership.

Driskel's longtime friend and chief Lieutenant, Stephen Brody, also helped continue the syndicate for a short time. Related by marriage to the Driskels four different ways, Stephen "Cropped Ears" Brody made up the other half of the gang, raising seven children of his own. "Cropped Ears" earned his nickname by having both ears cropped, the penalty at the time for third offense horse theft in Ohio. Around the time Driskel was arrested for stealing a candlestick, Brody had his first high profile brush with the law.

After Stephen Brody was involved in stealing local livestock, the local Constable secured an arrest warrant. When the Constable went to take Brody into custody, Brody decided not to go peacefully and stabbed him in the thigh. It earned Brody a three-year trip to the Ohio Penitentiary. Brody and his family, who were associates-in-crime of the Driskels for years, fled to Iowa after the execution of John and William. The Brody side of the gang consisted of John Brody Sr. and his sons John, Stephen, William, and Hugh.

They arrived in Benton County, Iowa in 1839, becoming some of the first pioneers of the area. Like the Driskels, John Brody[7] was originally from the Ashland area of Ohio. This is just north of Mansfield, where Driskel originated, and southwest of where the James Brown Gang operated in Summit County. Once in Benton County, the Brody family quickly claimed nearby Cedar, Jackson, and Linn counties as territory for their new branch of the outlaw gang.

After arriving in Benton County, Iowa, the Brody family quickly wore out their welcome, just as they did everywhere else. Just like in other reports, an honest man would not dare travel at night or leave a horse out to pasture in the evening, as it would be stolen in no time at all. The citizens in Jackson, Cedar, and Linn Counties lived in the same type of fear that the Driskels caused in Ogle County. It wasn't long before Regulators began forming in Iowa as well to deal with the outlaws who began to settle there. Historical records from Benton County report the same problems that were occurring in other Blackleg territories: the outlaws were difficult to capture and they would frequently escape from justice. Just as they did in Indiana and Illinois, some of the outlaws were among the ranks of the Regulators.

In April 1840, in nearby Jackson County, several members of the Brody Gang were involved in a very bloody shootout in a hotel owned by W.W. Brown. The incident started as a political dispute between Brown and rival Thomas Cox. The

---

[7] The Brody family had their name recorded as Broudy, Brodie, Brody and other variations.

dispute ended with one member of the gang killing a rival. Warrants were issued

and things went downhill from there. Brown and his men, including Aaron Long,

John Long, Granville Young, Richard Baxter, and others, were in town when

warrants were issued. When Warren, the local sheriff, went to serve the arrest

warrants, a crowd had already gathered and the liquor had been flowing for quite

some time.

Brown refused to go with the sheriff peacefully and resisted arrest, retreating

with his men into a hotel that he owned. They prepared themselves for war and the

shots began. What would later be known as the Bellevue War ended in a massacre.

Four of the drunken mob making the advance on Brown's hotel were killed and

three more were wounded. Brown and two others were killed inside the hotel. The

Long brothers, Young, Robert Birch, and two other men identified only by their

last names, Baxter and Chichester, were brought up on charges by Regulators

The Regulators at the time held a trial with beans. Using this method, each

person in the jury was issued two colored beans. One color meant the death

penalty, and the other meant lashings. Those in favor of lashings won and the men

were given between four and thirty-nine lashes each. They were then sent up the

Mississippi River with orders not to return under penalty of death.

As would later be learned in Rock Island, the men did not listen well. The

remaining members of the syndicate in Illinois continued their reign of terror on

the citizens, which expanded to include two murders. The first murder took place

in May of 1845 in Des Moines County, Iowa, and involved a local Mennonite man

named John Miller. There were rumors circulating that Miller had ten thousand dollars at his residence. Keep in mind that this was still in the era when banks were not federally insured, were frequently robbed, and were not as trusted as they are in today's society.

Among those in the syndicate who picked up on these rumors were William and Stephen Hodges, sons of Curtis Hodges Sr. of Nauvoo. Like many others in the mob family, the Hodges were previously residents of Ohio. Curtis Hodges was also known to dabble in trouble and may not have set the best of examples. By 1843, Curtis had been excommunicated from the Mormon Church by Brigham Young for "anti-Christian conduct," which occurred in Warrick County, Indiana. The Hodges were also closely connected with Lyman Johnson, who was one of the original leaders in the Latter Day Saints movement.

The Hodges, along with Blacklegs Thomas Brown and Aretemus Johnson, carefully planned the robbery of Miller and hit his residence around midnight one evening in May 1845. During the robbery Miller was murdered. Miller's son-in-law, Henry Leiza, was also wounded during the commission of the robbery. Leiza, who had been stabbed in the heart with a large bowie knife during the struggle, later died. The Sheriff was soon summoned and the manhunt began. One of the murderers was injured during the robbery and the posse was able to follow his trail to a nearby creek, and then back to the home of Grant Redden. By the creek, the Sheriff found a hat that was later identified as belonging to William Hodges.

Following the murders, the Hodges brothers returned to their hometown of Nauvoo, Illinois. It was there they met with William Smith, the brother of Joseph Smith. Nauvoo was a strong Mormon settlement and was also the home of Joseph

Smith, founder of the Latter Day Saints movement. When the Hodges arrived back in Nauvoo, they were not greeted with welcoming arms. William Smith ordered both brothers to leave Nauvoo and never return. Not satisfied with leaving, they sought out the advice of another influential Mormon named Brigham Young. Young's advice was that both brothers should turn themselves in to the police. Apparently they did not take such advice kindly, as they threatened to kill both William Smith and Brigham Young.

Needless to say, the brothers did not follow the advice of Smith or Young. Within days, the Sheriff of Lee County had their house surrounded and both brothers were taken into custody. They were brought to West Point and ordered to stand trial for the murders of Miller and Leiza. Fellow Blacklegs, including sympathizer Lyman Johnson, came to their aid and hired top-notch attorneys to prepare a defense. By this time Lyman Johnson had already been excommunicated from the Mormon Church. The defense strategy was to have at least three witnesses testify that the Hodges were both in Nauvoo, Illinois the day Miller and Leiza were murdered, and therefore could not have been in Des Moines, Iowa. Three of those witnesses were identified as Aaron Long, John Long, and William "Judge" Fox. This would not be the last time the names of those witnesses would surface in Blackleg history.

The Hodges' trial was held in June of 1845. During the trial an angry mob of Germans formed and threatened to take both men from custody and handle justice themselves. Cooler heads prevailed and the trial continued. After three days the jury came back with the verdict: "We the jury, find the defendants, William Hodges and Stephen Hodges guilty of murder." After being given an opportunity to speak, the sentence was pronounced: "That you be taken to the Jail whence you came, and remain there until the 15th day of July." It was on that day at 4 o'clock that both Hodges were sentenced to "be hanged by the neck until you are dead." The men were then sent to serve their remaining days at the prison in Alton, Illinois.

Upon hearing the news, a third brother of William and Stephen Hodges named Irwin (aka Ervine) did not take the news well. Irwin openly threatened to expose a number of crimes involving the Mormons unless Brigham Young were to take the lead in securing the freedom of his brothers. Like any true organized crime family, there was a code of silence that is never broken. Hodges was eventually tracked down into a field by Blackleg Return Jackson Redden where he was gutted with a bowie knife. Though it seemed to be well known that Redden was the Blackleg that took Irwin's life, no charges were ever filed, citing a lack of evidence.

With two Hodges brothers behind bars and the third brother dead, it seemed that the Blacklegs would lay low for a while. However, that was not the case. The Hodges had a fourth brother named Amos, who was part of the same group. Amos Hodges, along with Robert Birch and William Fox, prepared their next robbery against a local merchant named Rufus Beach. How Brigham Young found out about the planned robbery will likely never be known, but nevertheless Young tipped off Beach to the impending robbery. Beach in turn hired armed guards to protect his property. The robbery was thwarted and the men fled. Amos Hodges was eventually taken into custody but was bonded out by Mormon leader

Return Jackson Redding, Blackleg suspected of the murder of Irwin Hodges (not in copyright)

William Smith. Hodges was never heard from again.

In July of 1845, the Sheriff of Lee County, Iowa was authorized to spend fifteen dollars on new rope to hang William and Stephen Hodges and $400 to plan the entire event. The men rode in a wagon, along with their coffins, to the scaffold, where they met with four clergymen. After a short prayer and another denial of their crimes (to which they had once confessed), a cap was drawn over their faces and the Sheriff cut the rope that held them in suspense. Both men were hung by the neck in front of an estimated crowd of 10,000 onlookers in Burlington, Iowa. One account stated that the men were waiting until the last minute to be rescued by fellow Blacklegs, which may have been the reason they never made any last minute confessions.

By all accounts, Lyman Johnson, Curtis Hodges, and their close associates had all either been excommunicated from the Mormon Church or left it voluntarily. Their lack of association with the church did not stop many in the area from associating those men with the Mormon religion, however. There are some references that the men involved in these crimes were referred to as the "Old Mormon Banditti." Anti-Mormon feelings arose in the community and men began to run for public office specifically citing their stance against that religion.

Blacklegs from the same group then planned their next robbery and murder. It took place in Rock Island County and became one of the highest profile murders in the early days of Illinois. It involved some of the same men whose names we have heard several times in the past: John Long and his brother Aaron, along with Robert Birch, William Fox, John Baxter, Grant Redden, William Redden, and

Granville Young. They were all either indicted as accessories to murder, or directly charged with the murder of Colonel George Davenport.

During the robbery, they made off with a double barrel shotgun, a gold watch, and an estimated $600. The men who planned the robbery were under the impression that Davenport had over $10,000. There is no evidence that the men had planned to murder Davenport. Most accounts indicate that a gun accidentally went off during the robbery and shot Davenport in the thigh. After the shooting, the men escaped with what valuables they were able to find. Davenport's desperate pleas for help were finally answered, but his rescuers were unable to save his life. The family of Davenport offered a handsome $1500 reward to the person or persons who could find those involved.

The outrage over Davenport's murder did not afford the accused their freedom for long. The reward was enough to get the attention of famous detective Edward Bonney and a number of bounty hunters from all over the region who looked to cash in on the reward. Bonney was familiar with many of the characters involved and went undercover to track them down one by one. Fox was caught in Indiana but escaped custody before he was returned to Rock Island. Birch and Long were arrested near Fremont, Ohio. Birch escaped custody but did not

Colonel William Davenport, namesake of Davenport, Iowa, murdered by members of the Driskel Gang on July 4, 1845 (not in copyright)

last long on the run. He was killed three months later. Young fled with Davenport's gun and was captured near Fort Madison, Iowa. Aaron and John Long, along with their associate Granville Young, were all found guilty of murder.   At 11:00 AM on October 19, 1845, the Long brothers and Young were escorted by guards to the gallows. A crowd estimated at around 5,000 had gathered in the rain to witness the execution. The three men were well dressed and appeared calm while awaiting their fate. After the sheriff read their death warrant, each man was given the opportunity to say a few final words. John Long proclaimed that his brother Aaron and

Granville Young were innocent. John admitted to killing Davenport but claimed it had been unintentional. Long's final confession upon the gallows confirmed what we now know. He estimated that at that time there were already over two hundred men involved in the syndicate in Illinois, Indiana, and Missouri, as well as territories that had yet to be granted statehood. It was only when the men made their final approach to the rope that

JOHN LONG.

Sketch of John Long, accused murderer of Colonel George Davenport (not in copyright)

they displayed any kind of reaction. John Long was described as being quite calm, while the other two men were shaking with pure fear. Their arms were bound and blindfolds were then placed over their heads. The ropes were placed tightly around the necks of the accused before the floor fell from underneath them.

John Long and Granville Young fell a distance of four feet and were instantly hanged. The rope around the neck of Aaron Young, however, broke. This caused him immense pain; not only was he strangled for the short time before the rope snapped, but he struck his back against the structure as he fell. He proclaimed his innocence repeatedly while the guard found a replacement rope and walked him back up to the top of the gallows next to his brother, who was already hanging. Some of the witnesses in the crowd began to show mercy, asking the guards to let him go. Some feared that fellow Blacklegs were in a full rescue operation and began to flee. A still visibly shaken and now bloodied Aaron Young had to wait a second time for the inevitable. The new rope was placed around his neck and he was the last of the men to be executed. Grant Redden was brought to trial but not convicted, on account of one juror who did not believe he was guilty of the crime of which he was accused. Two of the remaining men accused of being involved in the murder of George Davenport were sentenced to unspecified prison terms. A number of Regulator incidents occurred over the next twenty years, most of them by associates of Driskel and Brody. There were a number of people ordered out of the country by Regulators and some attempted lynchings. It was a time of great unrest in eastern Iowa. One thing was noted, when the lynching started, that the Brodys themselves became very quiet and covert.

The Hanging of Granville Young, John Long, and Aaron Long, as illustrated in Edward Bonney's 1850 book, Banditti of the Prairies (not in copyright)

In the spring of 1857, Edward Soper, his associate Alonzo Gleason, and three others in the syndicate broke into the house of a German immigrant named Pennygrot near Louden, Iowa. A testament to the crime problem of the day, Pennygrot had actually been sleeping in his barn earlier in the night, as many pioneers did to ensure that their horses would still be stabled in the morning. Otherwise, the horses would undoubtedly be stolen sometime during the night. He was not in the barn upon the arrival of Soper, who quickly stole the horses. Soper and associates intended to move the horses east toward the Mississippi, into Illinois where the herd would move undetected through a series of safe houses.

While Gleason and Soper were still on the run, a new Regulator named William Corry identified a local horse thief named Alonzo Page. History now shows that it was unlikely Page was an actual horse thief, but the accusations were lodged due to a personal dispute between him and Corry. Regulators arrived at Page's house on the night of June 18, 1857. The Regulators present gave one of their famous "leave or else" warnings. When Page refused to leave, the windows and doors in his house were broken. He was shot and killed. The shot was believed to have been fired by Corry.

On July 2, 1857, information came in on the whereabouts of Gleason and Soper. During the pursuit of Gleason, Regulators came across another Blackleg named Peter Conklin. Regulators reportedly shot and killed Conklin, who was on the run and wanted on a $200 reward. There were later reports disputing his death. The sheriff of Linn County eventually moved in and arrested Soper before the Regulators could find him. Gleason was taken into custody shortly thereafter. They were both lodged in the county jail under tight security. The security was not tight enough for the Regulators, however.

That same evening, Regulators made their move and took Soper and Gleason out of jail, transporting them to one of the Regulators' farms where they would find a different kind of justice. The men were given a jury trial before twelve men and witnessed by over two hundred local residents. Obviously the men were found guilty after making full confessions. The trial immediately moved to the penalty phase, which was decided by those witnessing the trial. Both men were sentenced to death, and the execution was scheduled to be carried out the following day. On

July 3, 1857, the men were taken out to a large oak tree where ropes were placed around their necks. The men stood on the backs of wagons where they made their final remarks. The wagon was then moved from underneath them and they were executed for their crimes.

The account written of the execution seems very biased and was likely written by one of the Regulators themselves in order to justify their vigilante action. The description of the trial portrays it as being very fair, although that was likely not the case, as it was with most other Regulator trials. It records Gleason's last words as "Boys, I hope I'll meet you all in hell." Other records from the History of Cedar County describe the condemned men as cooperative, providing the names of thirty of their fellow outlaws in a futile effort to have their own lives spared.

In November of 1857, former Indiana resident and Blackleg Hiram Roberts was identified by Regulators as being another associate. Roberts began receiving threats from Regulators and decided he would try for leniency by turning himself in. Roberts was apprehended by a small number of Regulators and transported to nearby Jones County, Iowa. One of the Regulators present, who remains unidentified, was an employee of the Justice of the Peace in Linn County.

The Regulators began one of their trials in typical fashion. Several of the Regulators removed themselves from the barn where the trial was held to discuss the situation without the presence of the accused. The employee of the Justice of the Peace realized that the accused would not stand a chance of having a fair trial and would not be going before the judge of an established court. When the employee decided to leave, he went to retrieve his horse from the barn where the trial was to be held, only to find that Roberts's trial was already over and he was hanging from the beam.

Six of the men who were inside the barn were brought up on charges in Jones County for the death of Roberts. Obviously the only witnesses to the hanging of Roberts were the Regulators themselves, who had the full support of the community at the time. It was the prominent members of the community who had banded together to fight crime, versus a group of outlaws who had long terrorized the community. Not surprisingly, the jury was sympathetic to the Regulators. All six walked out of the courtroom free men after no indictment was found against them.

ANOTHER HORSE THIEF HANGED.—We learn from the Anamosa Eureka that Hiram Roberts, the notorious counterfeiter and horse thief, who was arrested at Red Oak Grove, in Cedar county, on Friday last, by the "regulators," was taken into Jones county, near Walnut Fork, and after having been tried and pronounced guilty, was hanged to a tree. His dead body was found on Saturday still hanging, having been left by the lynchers to be interred by others. Roberts, we believe, is the eleventh victim to 'lynch' law in the central counties of Iowa during the present year. The strange infatuation that has prompted the taking of life in this manner for an offence which the law does not punish with death will ever be an inexplicable disgrace to the fair fame of this state.—*Muscatine (Iowa) Fair.*

Account of the lynching of Hiram Roberts from the Daily Morning Gazette, Janesville, Wisconsin. (not in copyright)

105

10. MCDOUGALL'S EARLY YEARS

His name was recorded many different ways throughout the years.
McGregor, Gregory, "Blackhawk," or Gregor McDougall was born in 1831, the
son of Scottish immigrant Lachlin W. McDougall and Eliza Mary McGregor.
Gregor was born in Wallaceburg, a town bisected by the Sydenham River and
located near the small industrial city of Chatham, Ontario. It is through McDougall
that we can gain insight as to how an outlaw is made.

By all accounts, Gregor McDougall had a fairly normal upbringing. He was
the youngest of six children born over a span of fifteen years. The offspring of
Lachlin and Mary McDougall were John, Angus, Miles, Mary Ann, Lachlin Jr. (also
known as Lorne), and Gregor. Gregor's father Lachlin (sometimes spelled
Laughlin) was born in 1791 in Scotland. He arrived in Canada with his parents and
fourteen other families on the ship *Oughton* as part of the Baldoon Settlement in
southwestern Ontario.

The son of John and Sarah (McPherson) McDougall, Lachlin was held in
fairly high regard, working as a local merchandiser and an inn keeper. Gregor
McDougall's mother came from a good family as well. She was the daughter of
John McGregor, a War hero in the Kent Militia. John McGregor was a highly
respected veteran of the War of 1812, where he had lost an arm during battle. The

City of Wallaceburg itself was plotted on the estimated 800 acres of land given to the McGregor family by the Canadian government as a reward for his service and duty to country.

Exactly what went wrong with Gregor McDougall may never be known. It may have been youthful indiscretions, lack of discipline, or a variety of other possibilities. According to his own accounts, Gregor's parents were God-fearing, respectable people who gave him every opportunity in life. He admittedly did not take advantage of what was offered to him. Gregor appeared to have started his adult life on the right path, working in his father's merchandise business and running his own tavern for around two years. However, running a business in the small town of Wallaceburg did not give young Gregor the excitement he sought in life.

For that matter, pioneer days in Wallaceburg were not much more exciting for any of Gregor's brothers, as Gregor was not the only member of the McDougall family to dabble in trouble. Records show that all of them were involved in stealing horses and various other crimes. There are some reports that his brother Lachlin McDougall, believed to have gone by the name Lorne, was one of the chief operators in the crime syndicate. Lorne was identified by Canadian writer Rowland Whittet as being in charge of the transportation division of an outlaw gang which was dubbed the "Missouri, Illinois and Eastern Trading Company," described as operating from Canada through Missouri. In 1847 authorities eventually built a strong case against Lorne for stealing horses, and a warrant was soon issued for his arrest. During his arrest at his cousin's house,

Lorne resisted authorities and was able to wrestle away the pistol of the local constable, who was affecting the arrest. He was charged with stealing horses, with an added charge of assault with intent to commit murder. The constable was shot during the struggle but survived his wounds.

Lorne was found guilty and sentenced in May of 1848 to an eight-year prison term in the Kingston Penitentiary. During an interview with Lorne, conducted while he was serving time, he once claimed he was the head of the transportation division of the syndicate. He bragged of operating a stow, a boat capable of hiding as many as twenty stolen horses.

Growing up the youngest of the children, Gregor was highly influenced by all of his brothers' actions, including Lorne's. He carefully watched how each of them spent their own lives: stealing horses, robbing others, and leading the outlaw lifestyle. They lived exciting lives running from authorities and seeing the countryside of pioneer Ontario. This was compared to the life of his father, who routinely worked long hours every day and faithfully attended church every Sunday. He was also influenced by a man named William Townsend of the "Townsend Gang," who had been through Wallaceburg on numerous occasions. Townsend had recruited McDougall at a soldier level in the syndicate.

When his father died in 1852, McDougall was still living in Canada. Gregor's bond with his brothers grew closer after his father passed. After seeing his brother Miles arrested and locked up in the local jail, Gregor was at a crossroads in his life. He had to decide which way his life would turn. Would he follow the footsteps of his father as a respectable businessman, or would he become an outlaw like all of his brothers and become one of Townsend's men? His father was no longer around to influence the decision.

Gregor finally decided he would not sit idly by while his brother sat behind bars for stealing horses. Family ties being strong, Gregor hatched a plan to spring his brother from jail, which appears to have been the turning point in his life. Although Gregor did not realize the gravity of his decision, his life would never be the same.

By his own admission, Gregor went with his eldest brother John and their cousins to the jail in Chatham where his brother was lodged. Gregor and John climbed a ladder staged along the east wall of the jail. Once inside the yard the men busted in the door to the jail and found an elderly woman, the wife of the local jailor. Gregor denied that the jailor's wife was touched during the jail break. By his account she simply handed over the keys. McDougall would later be accused of murdering the woman, an accusation that he denied up until the last moments of his life.

Once the keys were in hand, the woman also handed Gregor a bag, which he described as being heavy. He denied knowing the contents of the bag, although this account is questionable. Once Gregor had the bag in hand he was confronted by more than one guard inside the jail. The other outlaws, who included Gregor's eldest brother John, immediately fled upon meeting the guards. Gregor was steadfast and threatened to start shooting if Miles was not released. The excitement was apparently too much for young Gregor, as he admitted to almost passing out during the jail break. He claims that after realizing the bag in his hand was full of gold, he returned the contents to the woman and fled with his brother Miles. There is no doubt he broke his brother out of jail. However, it is highly questionable that he would return a bag of gold once he had it in his hands.

Thus began the outlaw and fugitive life of Gregor McDougall, one that would later cut his life short. Not too long after the jail break, constables in the area obtained an arrest warrant for Gregor. In a letter that was intercepted by Regulators in Indiana, John warned Gregor that his liberty was at risk and his arrest was imminent. As soon as word got to him, Gregor knew he was in over his head. He packed up his belongings as quickly as possible and tried to get out of the area. He did not get very far before he found himself being pursued. McDougall traveled over twenty miles with the guards in pursuit. He made a successful escape, finding his way to Chemung County, New York. Unfortunately for his brother, Miles's life on the run did not last long. In August of 1854, Miles was arrested by the constable in Brantford, Ontario for robbing locals named Amos Shaw of Chatham and Henry Sharp of Dawn Township. By March of 1855, Miles was received into the penitentiary in Kingston, Ontario to serve a fourteen-year prison sentence on the charge of burglary and stealing horses. Miles stayed in prison up until his pardon on May 23, 1868. No explanation has ever been provided how Miles managed to obtain his pardon.

Once Gregor McDougall found his way to New York, he met with Sherman Mallet, the son of Erie and Sarah Mallet. They made their way along the Canadian border to St. Clair County, Michigan, where McDougall was married to fourteen-year-old Margaret Jacobs on July 11, 1852. Jacobs was born near Chatham on the

River Thames, daughter of Philip and Catherine (Parsons) Jacobs. Leaving Michigan, they made their way down to northeast Indiana to the small village of Burr Oak in Noble County, where they settled. Burr Oak is located just south of the former county seat of Noble County in Port Mitchell. McDougall bought a house next to Mallet and spent his first few weeks fixing things up. Undoubtedly Mallet was already involved in crime at this point. Mallet rented a horse from a nearby livery stable and traveled to the neighboring village of Port Mitchell, where he broke into a store. The stolen goods were partially lost in the Tamarack, which is near the county line where Noble and Lagrange counties meet. The rest of the goods were sold to the men's new acquaintance named William Latta, the same Latta who fled Summit County and was a close associate of Jim Brown as well as being connected by marriage to the Sturdivant clan from Cave-in-Rock.

There may have been a reason McDougall picked Noble County to make his settlement. If the man known in Noble County as Bill Hill was in fact William Townsend, McDougall would already have had a contact in the area, and this may have influenced his decision. Even if Townsend and Hill were not the same person, Noble County had already developed a nationwide reputation for being a den of horse thieves, counterfeiters, and other misfits. When McDougall arrived, he already had a job lined up within the syndicate.

Early postcard of the Kingston Penitentiary in Kingston, Ontario, Canada (not in copyright)

11. EARLY INDIANA ACTIVITY

The Blacklegs' reign of terror in Indiana began well before McDougall ever arrived in the area. It started even before the arrival of pioneers George Ulmer, William Latta, and William "Bill" Hill, which occurred around 1843. The network was already in place when McDougall was just a baby, growing up with his family in distant Wallaceburg. As soon as the settlement of northwest Indiana began, bands of thieves began organizing in the area.

Author Weston Goodspeed reported in his History of Noble County that the first efforts to clean up the region of horse thieves occurred upon the issuance of twenty arrest warrants in 1839. McDougall had not even reached the milestone of his tenth birthday when these first attempts at quashing Blackleg activity were made. Approximately twelve Blacklegs were identified by a thief, who decided to turn state's evidence in return for favorable treatment.

The arrested men were held and tried at Stone's Tavern, a few miles south of Ligonier, Indiana. There was immediate talk amongst the citizens against a formal trial. The citizens wanted to take matters into their own hands and lynch all of the horse thieves. Eventually those present left justice in the hands of the system, and

Tavern at Stone's Trace, Ligonier, Indiana. Courtesy of the Stone's Trace Historical Society

the Blacklegs received legal representation from attorneys Ewing and Breckenridge from Fort Wayne. The accused faced Judge Nelson Prentiss over the course of ten days. A good example of how justice worked back then was by the organization of this trial alone. Noble County did not have a prosecutor to offer up to represent the citizens. Luckily, an attorney just happened to be passing through from Piqua, Ohio. The locals sought his services and he graciously accepted. The initial efforts at ridding Noble County of its pioneer outlaws quickly turned disastrous. Two prisoners being held in Goshen, Indiana, were released on a technicality due to a problem with the paperwork. Some suspect the supposed "technicality" was

Judge Nelson Prentiss, from the History of Noble and Whitley
Counties *(not in copyright)*

more likely to have been a lenient judge on the payroll of Blacklegs. Seven others

who were being held in Fort Wayne, Indiana, broke out of jail and quickly fled the

area. Justice was never found during this first round of arrests.

Blacklegs resorted to the use of retaliation and intimidation in their pioneer

version of terrorism against anyone who would dare cross them. Two of the

pioneers who helped build a case against the accused at Stone's Tavern soon found

their barns burned to the ground by arsonists. The corruption in the justice system

only encouraged Blacklegs to continue on with business as usual. Getting arrested was not even a thought in the minds of these outlaws, as the construction of the jails meant escape could be accomplished with ease. The citizens were devastated at the failure in the justice system that occurred at Stone's Tavern. For most, it meant a return to sleeping in their barns, with guns ready day and night. It would be almost twenty years before a second attempt was made to rid the area of the criminals who plagued the entire region.

Although most references to Blacklegs describe them as horse thieves, they were involved in a multitude of other crimes. Just like the prohibition gangsters, their criminal enterprises involved burglaries, robberies, counterfeiting, extortion, arson, murder, and other crimes. There were also rumors of prostitution and organized gambling. Most of these crimes are serious felonies even in today's system, but they were especially devastating during the era of the Blacklegs.

To fully understand the gravity of the Blacklegs' actions, their activity must be viewed through a lens from the mid 1800's. A horse being stolen in 1850 was a much more serious affair than a car being stolen today. Horses were used for much more than transportation. A stolen car in today's world is a mere inconvenience. One quick trip to an insurance company will get most families back on the road. A horse served a much different purpose. It was a tool for farming, which fed pioneer families and served as a main source of income for most. A stolen horse could mean disaster for a pioneer family and could sometimes cost a person's life. It was one of the many risks of being a pioneer of that era.

During this time, Indiana was a true frontier and had been a state for less than fifty years. When the Blacklegs began their reign in the 1830's, the country did not extend any further than neighboring Illinois. Everything to the west was still unorganized territory. The southwestern part of the United States, including all of the area west of Colorado, was still part of Mexico.

The surroundings of northeast Indiana were much different than what we know today. Animals such as bears, elk, rattlesnakes, wolves, and panthers were commonly seen. Virgin timber forests were still being converted into usable farmland. Amongst other problems, law enforcement was minimal. Minor crimes were difficult enough to resolve and usually went unreported. Organized crime was well beyond the realm of anything that could be handled locally.

There have been a number of different branches of the organized crime network discussed throughout this book thus far. However, the true organization of these outlaws has not yet been covered. Make no mistake; this was not a group of dusty, uneducated outlaws who were friends based upon their mutual interest in stealing horses and passing a few counterfeit coins. In reality, the gang was far more organized and connected than anyone has ever acknowledged. Almost every scholarly resource for researching organized crime begins with Prohibition in the early 1920's. There are very few mentions of any such activity prior to 1900.

The extent of their organizational network was key in the long-term success of the Blacklegs. If a horse was stolen in Indiana, the thieves would be foolish to try to sell it anywhere in the same area. Instead, under the cover of darkness, the livestock and any other goods would be transported from state to state, eventually being sold hundreds of miles away to unsuspecting buyers. There are documented reports of barns with secret basements used to store stolen horses during their transportation throughout the Midwest. Blacklegs also used the region's ample swampland, which was much more prevalent during that time, for safe harbor. As previously mentioned, boats were also used to conceal stolen horses while they were transported more efficiently by water.

Nicknames were another trait shared between Blacklegs and the Prohibition Era gangsters. Just like "Baby Face" Nelson and "Lucky" Luciano, the Blacklegs coined names such as John "Flying Dutchman" Wilson, and Gregor "Blackhawk" McDougall. Their political connections at the highest levels of government were also a commonality. Their political reaches laid the groundwork for their counterparts nearly a century later. It was all the same: money, politics, bribery, intimidation, and every other trait that can be found in organized crime existed within the Blacklegs. As extensive as their activities were, the Blacklegs seem to be of a forgotten era in American History and have yet to be recognized as the founders of organized crime.

One major difference between Blacklegs and the gangsters of the Prohibition Era was in their cohesiveness. The organized crime families of the 1920's and 1930's were involved in a number of violent, bloody battles with fellow gangsters. They regularly killed each other in turf battles and petty personal disputes. This was not the case with the Blacklegs. The Blacklegs seemed to generally have a mutual respect for each other, regardless of territory, and there was really only one network. There is very little evidence of Blacklegs causing trouble for each other unless their own lives were being threatened, or under duress in some cases. This cohesiveness among the criminals undoubtedly made the job for law enforcement even more challenging. The only federal law enforcement authority at the time was the United States Marshal Service; however, their numbers were few and far between. There were less than a dozen Marshals that served Indiana in the 1850's, most of them serving for less than one year.

The Blacklegs' crimes were much easier to commit due to a lack of experienced Marshals and the inability of local law enforcement to cross state lines. There was also a lack of any modern crime scene investigative tools. Crimes such as burglaries and robberies could be executed with little difficulty. Fingerprinting technology and other crime scene investigative tools were only a dream back then. The only burglar alarm available existed in the form of a guard dog, which families might or might not have. Security lights only existed when the moon illuminated the night sky. The main form of communication at the time was the newspaper, which was sometimes only printed on a weekly basis. There were no phones to call the police, and no such thing as an emergency response.

Although Noble County did have a sheriff, his efforts were futile against the Blacklegs. The risk a sheriff would have undertaken to fight crime of this nature was also substantial. The sheriff was one man versus an entire army - not a task anyone in their right mind would have undertaken. The sheriff also faced a much more daunting task than being outnumbered by Blacklegs. A response from law enforcement would likely have taken hours, if not days. In addition, manpower would have been minimal for a rural Indiana county. It was unlikely that the office of the sheriff was even a full-time position.

First courthouse built in Noble County, Indiana from the <u>History of Noble County</u> by Weston Goodspeed (not in copyright)

It has already been established that many judges and attorneys only held those positions on the side. Their full time positions were running the local mill or farming the area fields. Responses were often delayed due to roads being rugged and impassible during any type of foul weather. These were prime conditions for

Blacklegs, who made their living victimizing others. Another issue was that by most accounts, the sheriff, constables, and other law enforcement were involved in the Blacklegs' activities. One corrupt link caused the entire system to fail.

According to the Noble County Sheriff's Department, the first jail in Noble County was not even constructed until 1849. Built out of logs, the security of the structure was an issue in and of itself, which contributed to the legacy of the Blacklegs, who regularly broke themselves out of jail. These jailbreaks occurred throughout all of northeast Indiana, not just in Noble County. This could be the reason why Regulators would later expeditiously serve as judge, jury, and executioner in the McDougall case. Leaving anyone in jail for any length of time meant that there was high risk of a breakout.

The size and extent of the Blacklegs' activities will likely never been fully known. Fact-finding is very difficult for several reasons, first and foremost being the passage of time. Over the course of time, many records have been destroyed or lost. Another reason is the nature of the story itself. This was an underground criminal network, so those involved were not exactly bragging about their activities. Criminals generally operated in secret to avoid capture. For this reason, Gregor McDougall and the Regulators are owed a debt of gratitude for precipitating the documentation of the criminal activity of the day, which is not recorded anywhere else.

12. INDIANA REGULATORS

What exactly is a Regulator? On March 9, 1852, the same year McDougall arrived in Indiana, the General Assembly of the State of Indiana recognized the problem at hand. They authorized the citizens of Indiana to form themselves into companies specifically for the purpose of detecting and apprehending horse thieves. The state gave specific requirements and guidelines that had to be obeyed. Regulator companies were required to register with the local Recorder's Office. Each member of the company and his place of residence were to remain public at all times. Amongst other guidelines, the companies were given the power to call for the assistance of the peace officers of the State in the pursuit and apprehension of felons. They also had the power to reclaim stolen property and arrest the offenders. They were given the same rights and privileges as the constables of the day. Throughout history there were Regulators authorized by state law and some who were no more than vigilantes who banded together. The general idea was the same, though, regardless of whether or not they were officially authorized.

By September the same year, the first band of Regulators was formed in northeast Indiana, identifying themselves as the Lagrange County Rangers. Recruiting Regulators was likely difficult at first, due to the retaliation which occurred after the trial at Stone's Trace years earlier. Any reluctance in joining, however, was quickly overpowered by the sense that something must be done. The ranks of the Regulators grew swiftly. The formation of the Lagrange County Rangers was quickly followed by the formation of a number of other companies, the membership of which exceeded five hundred in Noble County alone.

According to the History of the Regulators by M.H. Mott, their job dismantling the criminal element in the region was not an easy one. As previously mentioned, sheriffs, judges, attorneys, public officials at all levels, and other respectable members of the community were all connected to the Blacklegs. Even when a criminal was finally caught and arrested, their escape from jail was usually imminent. It was always a gamble whether or not the charges would actually stick.

On January 9, 1858, the Regulators published notice in the local newspaper, the "Lagrange Standard," outlining the intentions of the Regulators. They specifically targeted local tavern owner Benjamin Wilson, who operated near Wright's Corners in Lagrange County. The area formerly known as Wright's Corners is located north and slightly west of South Milford. Their resolution accused Wilson of being an accomplice, passing counterfeit money through his business, and providing safe haven for Blacklegs. The Regulators detailed their intentions to hold Wilson accountable, and the resolution was signed by over one hundred thirty supporting citizens. The display undoubtedly caused some level of nervousness amongst the Blacklegs, if only because this was the largest effort thus far to put a stop to their network. Those who authored the resolution were bold enough to draft it right in the same area of Wright's Corners. Their boldness was no doubt intended to send a message to the Blacklegs.

Following the signing and publishing of the resolution, a group of pioneers met in Kendallville, Indiana, on January 16, 1858. The meeting of the pioneers was known as the "Old Settlers' Meeting." Prior to the start of the meeting, more than three hundred men rode through Kendallville on horseback as a show of force. Riding through the dusty streets, the Regulators wanted to show the Blacklegs they would no longer live in fear. They reminded the citizens through a proud display of hand painted banners that the Regulators' activities were all volunteers and at no expense to the county. One banner boldly proclaimed, "Now we are ready to strike, for liberty or death."

The men who made up the Regulator force were the founders and average citizens of the area who would no longer tolerate being victimized at the hand of Blacklegs. The Regulator companies were comprised of farmers, local business owners, and ordinary citizens who had been living for decades in constant fear. As later determined, some of the Regulators were actually Blacklegs trying to get inside information on who was being targeted. Regardless of a few infiltrators, the honest Regulators were bound and determined to take their communities back from the Blacklegs. The Regulators made it known that they were willing to place their own lives on the line to accomplish their mission.

On January 17, 1858, the Regulators appointed James McConnell of the Regulator company "Noble County Invincibles" as head of a fifteen-man posse tasked to make the first arrests. Their first stop was Rome City, Indiana, in the northern part of Noble County. Gregor "Blackhawk" McDougall was on the top of the list. He was one of the first Blacklegs taken into custody by McConnell.

Reunion photo of the Regulators from Ligonier, Indiana. Photo originally published by the Ligonier Banner (1879-1950) and now hangs in the wall of the Dekalb County Courthouse. (not in copyright)

How exactly was McDougall identified and caught? The only evidence found thus far appears in the Fort Wayne Journal Gazette on December 10, 1911, by correspondent A.M. Groves. It was perhaps the best and most impartial investigation done, even though it was decades after the vigilante execution of McDougall.

It should be mentioned that the term "vigilante" is in no way a derogatory or accusatory term. If fact, the origin of this term comes from the word "vigilant," which was used by the Regulators themselves when coming up with names for their companies. Newspaper accounts which favored Regulator justice often

Regulator E.B. Gerber and his family from Noble County, Indiana. Gerber owned a hardware store in Ligonier. (Photo from Goodspeed's History of Noble County, (not in copyright)

referred to the organizations as "vigilance committees." Other, more light-hearted, accounts referred to the Regulators' activities as trials before "Judge Lynch." Groves interviewed several Regulators who were involved in the arrest of Blacklegs in January 1858. According to one Regulator named Charles Inks, the first progress by Regulators to disband the Blacklegs occurred when a member of the syndicate was caught selling stolen goods from a local farmer's smokehouse. The Regulators interviewed the man, who, when asked kindly to provide the names of other Blacklegs, replied "I'll be damned if I will." Unfortunately for this Blackleg, the Regulators' patience was worn. The man was later identified as Matthew Billings in an article that appeared in the *Fort Wayne Journal Gazette* on January 30,

1916. The account written by Groves provides more details on the involuntary confession obtained from Billings. Regulators reportedly brought Billings to the small village of Lisbon in Noble County and tied him to a post. They put one end of the rope around Billings' neck, and the other end was thrown over a rafter on the top of the building. The interrogators would lift Billings off of the ground by his neck until he would slowly lose consciousness. After each trip upward the Regulators would demand to know the names of his connections.

The *Journal Gazette* quotes the Regulators as repeatedly warning Billings, "Tell or we'll kill you," referring to their efforts to identify additional Blacklegs. Once his feet left the ground a few times, the slightly taller Billings made the wise decision to talk. It was through Billings' confession that McDougall and other Blacklegs were identified. According to the History of the Regulators, the first Blacklegs arrested were Miles C. Payne, Gregor McDougall, Sol Stout, Malcom Burnham, Joseph Hall, William Hall, E. Kesler, and Davis French. McConnell's posse was successful in its initial efforts to round up the members of this criminal network, which for long had terrorized the community.

One innocent man had a close call in Kendallville, Indiana. The *Allen County Democrat* reported that while the Regulators were making their initial arrests, an unidentified, respectable local man visiting Kendallville was awoken in the middle of the night by a band of Regulators who suspected him of being a Blackleg. He was questioned at length before it was determined that the man was not involved in Blackleg activity and was simply on the way to visit his soon-to-be bride.

Those who were arrested made the slow journey by horse and wagon

130

under the tightest security. Undoubtedly, those in custody must have had some

glimmer of hope that they would be saved by the system they had corrupted for so

long. There may have been a sense of confusion as well. They were arrested by

fellow citizens, not by anyone in the law enforcement system. There wasn't a

sheriff or Deputy Marshal in sight. Nobody had dared in decades to take any kind

of action against them, let alone the average citizen. They now found themselves

bound and shackled by farmers and businessmen.

Recall that the State of Indiana had only authorized the Regulators to detect

and apprehend. Under the color of law, the duties of the Regulators had been

fulfilled when they detected and apprehended those suspected of stealing and

counterfeiting. The Regulators therefore faced a most difficult decision. They did

not need a reminder that the criminal justice system remained corrupt to the core.

This corruption had to be on the minds of the Regulators as the first arrests were

Regulator John Bowman, farmer from York Township in Noble County. (Sketch from Goodspeed's History of Noble County, not in copyright)

The Work Goes Bravely On.—The work of "Regulation" is progressing in Lagrange county, and along the Plank Road A number of arrests were made at Avilla, Lisbon, and in that vicinity last week, and a detachment of the Regulators about the same time visited Albion, with a "Subpœna!' The result was that a citizen went forth—"witnessing" We understand that the Plank Road Committee have a heavy "docket" to go through and will probably be in active session for several weeks. At South Milford, in Lagrange county, they have a large number of the "l fers," "pullers" and "shovers" whose several cases are being duly and considerately attended to It is said that several women have been arrested in Lagrange, charged with active complicity in the nefarious operations of the gang—particularly in passing counterfeits We hope and believe, however, that the number of women whom it may be necessary to arrest will be very small The force of circumstances may, in a few instances, have drawn or driven women into such positions ; but in nine cases in ten it is so utterly repugnant to woman's native conscientiousness and inherent rectitude that they will rejoice at the revolution which releases them from the foul enthralment.—*Noble County Democrat.*

Report on Regulator activity from the Fort Wayne Sentinel, February 6, 1858 edition. (not in copyright) made. The Regulators were in a position where they could no longer trust the system to bring justice to those accused. The citizens debated at Stone's Tavern decades earlier about the means by which justice could be found. They ultimately trusted the system, which failed. They had been victimized for too long and knew action must be taken. Were they willing to take another chance with the rugged, corrupt criminal justice system versus a band of organized criminals?

Before any decision could be made by Regulators, they first had to complete their investigation and identify anyone else involved. Mott's history portrays the questioning and trial of McDougall as fair and impartial; however, other accounts were not as flattering. McDougall was described as a hardened, cold, and unapologetic criminal. Upon questioning, McDougall refused to cooperate or give up the names of any other Blacklegs. He told the Regulators he would not be intimidated by their actions. The Regulators decided to put his theory to the test. A rope was then placed around his neck for a short time and Regulators pulled him upward, just as they did in the questioning of Matt Billings. It was a clear message from the Regulators that a confession would be obtained through any means necessary.

The number of times McDougall's feet were raised above the ground was not documented. However many times it took, McDougall eventually decided that talking to the Regulators was his best, or only, option. He made a full confession of the crimes in which he and other Blacklegs in the area were involved. Perhaps it was a last ditch effort by McDougall to save his own life. After providing a full confession, McDougall awaited his fate. The Regulators took a vote and decided that the criminal justice system could not be trusted. The decision was made that McDougall would have his trial before a committee of Regulators, not in a court of law. The Regulators' trial for McDougall was held inside McClain's Hall, which was later the site of Citizens Bank in Ligonier, Indiana. The building stands today at the corner of Third Street and Cavin.

The questioning and trial of McDougall was effective, but obviously not up to legal standards or authorized under any other interpretation of the law. The Regulators were not only acting outside the scope of the authority given to them by the Indiana General Assembly, but also outside the rights afforded to each individual by the United States Constitution. Regardless, the Regulators felt they had no choice.

While the quasi-trial was being held, the Regulators benefited from the testimony of a Deputy U.S. Marshal identified as Halstead, who apparently wasn't concerned about the legalities of the trial. In addition to McDougall's confession, Halstead testified McDougall was wanted for two murders in Canada. There is no evidence McDougall was ever allowed to have witnesses testify on his behalf, refute any evidence presented, or even make any attempt to defend himself against the accusations brought forth by Regulators. Grove's article in the *Fort Wayne Journal Gazette* from 1910 describes the extent of the Regulators' distrust of the system. Upon hearing of the scheduled execution of McDougall, an attorney from nearby Albion, Indiana, attempted to intervene on McDougall's behalf. Although not identified, it is highly suspected this man was Hiram Tousley, who would later help the widow Margaret McDougall settle her husband's estate.

James McConnell, the Regulator who arrested McDougall, told the attorney, in a not-so-kind way, to either leave or he would find himself hanging alongside McDougall. This suggests the decision to hang McDougall had already been made prior to any trial before the committee. The only attempt by anyone to provide McDougall with a legitimate defense during his trial before the committee had failed. The attorney saved his own life by returning to Albion. The Regulators

Formerly known as Citizens Bank, the building located in Ligonier, Indiana was the site where Regulators held their trial of McDougall and other Blacklegs. (sketch not in copyright)

One lawyer who went from this city to endeavor to obtain the liberation of the accused, was looked upon as an accomplice, or at least as an aider and abettor of the scoundrels, and was summarily arrested and confined with his supposedconfederates. After being held in durance two or three days he was liberated, and *dodged* back at a 2.40 speed, a wiser and a better man, glad to find his neck unstretched, even though minus his expected fee. If this method of treating all who give aid and comfort to the rascals is rigidly carried out, we have strong hopes that the band will be thoroughly routed, and Noble county be effectually cleared of those who have been so long a terror and annoyance to its good citizens.

Excerpt from an article in the <u>Fort Wayne Sentinel</u> from January 23, 1858. The article is believed to be referring to Attorney Hiram Tousley. (not in copyright) made the conscious decision that they were the only individuals who could find true justice.

McDougall's trial began and ended on January 25, 1858. Regulator justice was swift, and the outcome is well documented. The findings and sentencing of the Central Committee were recorded as follows:

"We, the committee appointed by the Noble County Invincibles, to collect and investigate the evidence in the case of Gregory McDougle, now pending before the society, ask to make the following report: After having made a full and fair investigation of all the testimony, and having found, during said investigation, evidence of an unmistakable character, charging the said Gregory McDougle with murder, do recommend, that the said McDougle be hung by the neck until dead, on Tuesday, the 26th day of January, 1858, at 2 o'clock P.M."

Attorney Hiram Tousley of Albion, Indiana from the History of Noble County. (not in copyright)

McDougall was found guilty and sentenced to hang the following day. The Regulators immediately dispatched some of their members to notify McDougall's wife of the fate that awaited her husband. Upon hearing the news, McDougall's wife fainted and collapsed with their young daughter Ida in her arms. After she was revived, a tearful and devastated Margaret McDougall threw herself on the mercy of the Regulators who guarded her husband. She begged them to hold off on his scheduled execution long enough to prove he was innocent of the murder charges. Her pleas fell upon deaf ears. In less than twenty- four hours Margaret McDougall would be a widow and single mother in the rough world of pioneer Indiana. The Regulators would go forward with the scheduled execution the following day.

13. MCDOUGALL'S CONFESSION AND EXECUTION

The Blacklegs' activities were so widespread and well known that the name and reputation of the residents in Noble County were soon tarnished nationwide. Goodspeed reported in 1882 that, during the infamous California Gold Rush, anyone claiming to be from Noble County was immediately met with a level of distrust. How bad a crime problem was caused by the Blacklegs?

The best account of the Blacklegs' criminal activities came from the confession of McDougall, which was recorded by Reverend Wolcott (namesake for the Town of Wolcottville, Indiana) in January of 1858. Although his criminal history seems extensive, there is not enough known to compare his history with other Blacklegs. The only reason we know so much about McDougall's crimes is because of his ill-fated demise. It is more likely that Blacklegs Perry Randolph, William Hill, William Latta, and George Ulmer were involved in far more crimes than McDougall. These men arrived in the area from Summit County, Ohio, over a decade before McDougall. They started their lives of crime when McDougall was just a little boy. However, their confessions were never recorded in Mott's publication of Regulator activities, as they were all still on the run at the time the book was written.

Mott's details and chronicle of Blacklegs may have been skewed to protect the interests of the Regulators at the time. Regardless, let there be no doubt that Gregor McDougall was an outlaw and a criminal. We know of his involvement in the jailbreak in Chatham, Ontario. Breaking his brother out of the jail was only the tip of the iceberg. It appears that the rest of McDougall's life of crime occurred after he arrived in Indiana. McDougall relayed criminal exploits which were recorded prior to his death in the following confession:

Within six weeks of his arrival in the region, McDougall was approached by William Latta near Burr Oak, Michigan. Latta offered to provide counterfeit money to McDougall and Sherman Mallet. At the time, Latta was operating a hotel and tavern near the now defunct village of Freedom. The village was located east of Sturgis along the Chicago turnpike, which is now known as U.S. 12. Latta's hotel had a reputation for being a den of horse thieves and counterfeiters.

As a side note, there is further evidence supporting the idea that McDougall was not in a leadership position of the syndicate, as he would later be accused. Latta's hotel had a very violent reputation prior to the time McDougall ever arrived in the area. On October 30, 1848, authorities in Indiana were seeking a horse thief from Mississippi by the name of Ward, who found Latta's hotel a comfortable place to rest while on the run. In pursuit were three members of a posse, including Constable Gamamiel Fanning[8]. During a search of Latta's property, Fanning found Ward lying on the ground next to a large log. When Fanning confronted Ward, the suspect jumped up with a large knife and plunged it through the chest of the constable. Fanning's life ended that same day. Ward once again went on the run

---

[8] Fanning is believed to be the first law enforcement line of duty death in the State of Michigan

and was found a mere thirty minutes later hiding in the woods. He was charged with the murder of Fanning and sentenced to fifteen years in prison. Ward's sentence ended six years into his imprisonment, when he died.

The attention brought to Latta's hotel did not discourage him from continuing on with the syndicate. Upon McDougall's arrival to the region, Latta used the opportunity to create new business deals. In exchange for providing McDougall with counterfeit, Mallet and McDougall needed to be willing to buy various goods with the money. McDougall took Latta up on the offer. He went on a trip with Mallet over to a dry goods store in Elkhart County, which they robbed. They made off with about $300 worth of stolen property, a good haul for that era, which they brought back with them to Burr Oak. Some of the goods were sold to another Blackleg named Jeremiah Misner. The remaining goods were given to Latta and Randolph, in exchange for counterfeit money.

McDougall took some of that counterfeit money on a trip up to Detroit, Michigan, and met with other members of the syndicate. He went with Mallet, his brother John McDougall, and a Blackleg named William Ray. After they rolled into town, McDougall and associates passed about sixty dollars worth of the bogus money. McDougall admitted he still had about eight hundred dollars worth of counterfeit in his pocket, some of which he sold to Mallet. He then hired a few horses in Romeo, Michigan, and took them to Mallet's hometown in Chemung County, New York, where they were sold to a Blackleg named Edward Howard.

McDougall returned to Indiana and met with Perry Randolph near Kendallville. While he was visiting with Randolph, McDougall had his first brush with the law in Indiana. Upon returning home, he found that the sheriff of Noble County had already searched his house (with or without a warrant) and was awaiting his return. For whatever reason, the sheriff did not arrest McDougall, and he left town two hours later. This was a pivotal point in McDougall's life, as he admits that it was during this visit by the sheriff that his wife first learned of his connection to organized crime.

After his brief brush with the law, McDougall returned home to Wallaceburg, Ontario, Canada. This is an interesting stop, as he would later be accused of murders that happened in Wallaceburg. If he was in fact wanted for murder, stopping anywhere near this area would have been highly unusual and dangerous for an accused murderer on the run.

He stole a few horses in Wallaceburg and took them to London, Ontario, where they were sold. He spent the winter running through Canada and New York stealing horses and harnesses, as many as he could find to make it through the winter. He identified that he spent part of the winter with a Blackleg named William "Bill" Hill, who of course is suspected of being Townsend. He returned home to Burr Oak after the Christmas of 1856, but just for a short time. He soon began traveling back to Wallaceburg with his wife and cousin, stealing horses all along the way. After visiting Wallaceburg, McDougall returned to familiar Blackleg territory in Chemung County, New York.

Once again, he found himself in the company of Edward Howard. They both plotted to rob a man known as Big Jim. McDougall and Howard went into Big Jim's house, where they used chloroform to knock him unconscious. After Big

Jim was out cold, they robbed him of ninety-five dollars and a gold watch. McDougall kept the watch and twenty bucks, while his accomplice Howard kept the rest.

While in New York, McDougall met up with Mallet in Chemung County. Mallet had just been pardoned and released from prison in Canada, where he had been serving time in the Kingston Penitentiary. Mallet's time in prison apparently did not teach him much; at their next stop in Jefferson, New York, they broke into a drug store and stole some jewelry, pocketknives, and cash.

After selling off the goods, their next stop was the village of Penn Yan, New York. They broke into a store, stealing hundreds of dollars worth of tea and tobacco. This was followed by a stop in Ellicottville, New York, where they stole a few horses and wagons. It was during this trip they met with another Blackleg named Phipps. This is believed to be Eli or John Phipps. McDougall held the horses while Phipps and Mallet severely beat and robbed a man by the name of Oxen. Whether he actually just held the horses or was a more active participant in the crime will never be known. McDougall and Mallet slowly made their way across Ohio and stopped in Tiffin (Seneca County), where they sold all of the stolen goods to a local peddler.

When McDougall made it back to Indiana, he began associating with a Blackleg named Malcom Burnham. He received a total of thirty dollars in counterfeit coins from Burnham and $2000 in counterfeit money from Bill Hill. McDougall took this money to Chautauqua, New York. Upon his return to Burr Oak, Michigan, McDougall met up with Miles Payne, the man who would later be

143

State of Indiana)ss In the LaGrange Circuit Court
LaGrange County)   October Term AD 1858

State of Indiana)
        vs   )
Miles Payne   ) The Grand Jury of the County
of LaGrange and State of Indiana duly
empaneled Sworn and Charged in the
LaGrange Circuit Court at its October term
AD 1858 upon their oath present and charge
that Miles Payne late of said County on the
first day of September in the year of our
Lord Eighteen hundred and fifty seven at
the County of LaGrange and State of
Indiana aforesaid, one set of Double
harness of the value of Twenty five
Dollars of the personal Goods of one
Samuel P Williams then and there being
found, unlawfully and feloniously did
Steal take and carry away contrary to
the Statute in such case made and
provided and against the peace and
dignity of the State of Indiana
                        James H Schell
                        Special Pros atty
                        10th Circuit

Indictment of Miles Payne in Lagrange County, Indiana

arrested the same day as McDougall. McDougall and Payne stole a pair of horses from Wolf Lake and took them to be sold in Chautauqua, New York. They stole another pair of horses and sold them to Malcom Burnham.

Other Blacklegs soon entered McDougall's life, including Barney Weston and Sol Stout. Stout was also with McDougall when McConnell's posse made the first arrests. McDougall went with both men up to Springfield in Lagrange County, Indiana, and broke into a store where they stole about two hundred dollars in goods. Weston kept the goods, giving McDougall a wagon in exchange. McDougall in turn sold the wagon to Burnham for some extra cash. Payne and McDougall broke into a series of other stores, stealing boots, gloves, and anything else they could get their hands on.

During McDougall's confession, he admitted to stealing many more horses and wagons, and routinely involving himself in the trade of counterfeiting money. He implicated other Blacklegs by the names of Ed Kessler, Hadley, Smitzer, McKenzie, and Forsyth. In addition to all of the crimes in which he was personally involved, McDougall conceded his knowledge of many other crimes involving Blacklegs throughout northeast Indiana and the Midwest.

In Dekalb County, Indiana McDougall identified those involved in the burglary of a store in the small village of Spencerville. He also gave the names of two individuals who manufactured counterfeit money in Uniontown. McDougall also relayed his knowledge of the stabbing and robbing of a local man named Myers from that area. McDougall was not involved but identified the men responsible as Blacklegs Hadley and Hunt.

In Ligonier, Indiana, McDougall pointed out Hank Core as the person responsible for stealing a buggy. Although the Regulators reported his last name as Core, it is believed this person is actually Henry Gore, who was a local resident at the time. In addition, there was a store broken into by Charles Smith and another Blackleg identified only by his last name, Wilkinson. The goods from the robbery were sold to Bill Hill.

In Lagrange, McDougall pointed out the local constable named Carmie Lowther as dealing in counterfeit and stolen horses. Coincidentally, Lowther happened to be the constable who summoned the jury in the Sile Doty murder case over in Steuben County. James Pitts and Al Nimmons were both accused of printing their own money. John Goodrich[9] of Lagrange helped the Blacklegs by hiding horses on his property and also dealt in counterfeit money. Brothers Dan and Ben Wilson[10], local tavern owners, both dealt in the bogus funds and helped store stolen horses. McDougall implicated a local doctor by the last name of Hogan as being involved in counterfeit money.

Down in Fort Wayne, Indiana, McDougall accused local tavern owner Jed Cothrell of being involved in printing money. Cothrell would later be indicted for counterfeiting and taken into custody by U.S. Marshals. Cothrell, the owner of Mad Anthony's Saloon, regularly dealt in stolen goods and counterfeit money with Hill and Burnham.

---

[9]There is no listing of a John Goodrich living in Lagrange County in census records from that era, so the spelling may be incorrect.

[10]Wilson's Tavern is the location Regulators first identified in their resolution as being a haven for Blacklegs.

McDougall's knowledge of Blackleg activity was not limited to northeast Indiana. He knew of a Jonathon Thompson from Kinsman, Ohio, and Ott Hoken from the same area who both dealt in counterfeit currency. McDougall also worked with William Thompson, a former sheriff in New York, who knowingly dealt in fraudulent money. From that same area, McDougall worked with other men from the same family identified as John and Henry Thompson, as well as a tavern owner, Charles Hibbard, who were all knowingly involved in the crime syndicate. Finally, McDougall brought up the name of John Rosenkraus from Bath, New York, who dealt in counterfeit.

McDougall confessed to two other crimes, both robberies, but only after being specifically confronted by his accusers. The first robbery was in Wallaceburg, Ontario, where McDougall admitted to robbing a man named Alexander McCoy of his watch. This happened shortly after he broke his brother Miles out of the jail in Chatham. During the robbery, McCoy apparently fell on the ice but McDougall denied he was hurt. McDougall further related that McCoy was at his house the next morning for a drink.

The second robbery occurred in western New York, but was described by Troyer in his book "Salt and the Savor" as being in Indiana[11]. McDougall's involvement in this crime was limited. He was with Sherman Mallet and William Roy when they went to the home of an old Scotsman in the area. The old Scotsman was smoking a pipe when Mallet and Roy asked him for a drink. When the old Scot got up, Roy knocked him down and demanded all of his money. The

---

[11] Troyer portrayed the Old Scot as a neighbor of Blackleg Malcom Burnham.

old Scotsman said it was all in the bank. Mallet and Roy poured out all of the man's flour and wheat in search of any hidden money. Afterward, they put live coals in a kettle and placed it on the victim, but the Scotsman's story did not change. They robbed the man of a watch and fled. McDougall would only admit to holding the horses outside while this robbery took place, the same role he claimed to play in the previous robbery. He adamantly denied involving himself any further in the crime.

One point to make about McDougall's confession: it supports the idea this was an actual organized crime syndicate and not merely a bunch of loosely involved criminals. This was more than just selling off a few horses. If you read his confession carefully, McDougall states that he made a circuit from his new home in Indiana back to Ontario. Horses that were stolen in one area were transported back west, whereupon he would then work his way back east. The Blacklegs knew how to travel, where to stay, and where they could sell their stolen property without being detected. McDougall was nothing more than a soldier working in the field in this organized crime outfit. He was by no means a person who held any role of leadership.

McDougall was no doubt a hardened individual who lived his life robbing and stealing from others. These are only the crimes he recalled and admitted to after 1852, when his father died, up until 1858, when he was arrested. McDougall's confession shows the scope and extent of Blacklegs' reach. A Blackleg once noted that if the Regulators took ten random citizens, he could find one who knowingly dealt in counterfeit.

There are additional reasons why McDougall's account of his crimes is historically important. With the exception of Sile Doty's autobiography, it is one of the most comprehensive accounts of Blackleg activities. It brought forth a number of names of Blacklegs, which in turn resulted in numerous arrests and the disbandment of Blackleg activities in the region. Finally, it gives enough information that it can help us one hundred and fifty years later in deciding McDougall's guilt. The roots of the criminal element were very deep and widespread. The situation was desperate and the law-abiding citizens of the area had no choice but to act.

And so, it is January 1858, the day following his trial; the day of his hanging. Gregor McDougall, a young man in his mid-twenties and faced with immediate death, has reversed his harsh attitude and has asked to see his wife and child, a request which has been granted. The only solace for McDougall may be the knowledge that his daughter is far too young to ever recall the horror that is about to unfold.

Undoubtedly during this time, part of McDougall wished he would have stayed in rural Wallaceburg to continue running his father's business. Perhaps he wished he could turn back the clock and not enter the jail that held his brother with the intent of breaking him free. Perhaps McDougall regretted not living the life of a family man, raising his daughter and caring for his aging mother in a far more peaceful environment than where he currently stood. It is recorded that the family wept together before finally being forced to bid their final farewell.

McDougall was then escorted by one thousand armed men along the rutted winter road to Diamond Lake in Ligonier. He rode to the execution site in a wagon, which also carried the coffin that would later be used for his burial. The trip must have been dreadful for McDougall, knowing that the same coffin that he rode next to on the long journey to a violent end would be his prison for eternity.

It was a parade of sorts for the citizens of northeast Indiana, but the purpose was likely a show of force meant to serve as an intimidation factor to any Blacklegs who dared be witness. It was a message to the Blacklegs that there were now far more Regulators willing to put their necks on the line. It was a battle of good versus evil, and the law-abiding citizens were sure to prevail.

The following was recorded by Reverend Wert with Regulator A.B. Miller and details the final words given by McDougall in front of the crowd who witnessed his execution:

"I am happy to see such a crowd around me, and I hope that all young men will take a warning from me. My old father and mother advised me to do good. I never committed murder. They say that I killed a man and woman in Canada, and that I burnt a man to make him tell where his money was. It is false. The worst crime I committed was in New York. I then stole, and hurt a man, which long troubled me, but he got well. I have stolen many times and taken many horses. Mr. Braden [Regulator J.E. Braden] has my confession, which I am willing you all should see. I am sorry to be here, but it might as well be my life as another's. I say to young men, keep from houses of ill-fame, and instead of playing cards, read your bible. The first deviation is the worst. The progression is easy then to robbery, and finally to murder. No man, I think, has any hard feelings towards me, and I have hard feelings towards none. The citizens of Ligonier have treated me kindly. It is my unhappy portion that my doom should be a warning to all young men,

and I am glad to see so many here. It is said that I fear neither God, man, or the devil. I do fear

God. It is but a few years since I commenced this course. I broke jail in Canada to release my

brother. I was discovered and had to flee my country, and have since fallen into bad ways. I was

forced by circumstances into the society of bad men, and hence have pursued a bad course. There are

quite a number of people who think the Committee is mistaken in what they do. I say they are

not. They are justified, and I hope they will succeed in their undertaking, and root out all the

thieving, coining, counterfeiting, and horse stealing. Many present are probably as bad as me, but I

hope they will all, especially the young men, take warning by me. My only source is God. I trust to

Him for mercy. I trust in the Lord."

There are two accounts of the actual execution. The earliest account was reported by Goodspeed in his <u>History of Noble County</u>. Goodspeed reported that McDougall was placed on the back of a wagon and the rope was placed around his neck by a Regulator named Christian Heltzel. McDougall's hands were bound behind him and he was placed on a plank running from the end of a wagon, supported at the end by two posts. Upon receiving a signal, the wagon was pulled from underneath his feet and McDougall was hanged by the neck until dead. It was not an easy death by some accounts. His neck was not immediately broken and he struggled for about half an hour before passing away.

A different account of his execution was found in the January 30, 1916 edition of the *Fort Wayne Journal Gazette*. An eyewitness to the execution was interviewed for their report. The eyewitness relayed that one end of the rope was placed around McDougall's neck while the other end was placed around a tree. McDougall was then stood upon a box. The order was given to kick away the box, but nobody stepped forth for the dreaded task. After several minutes of silence, a witness stepped forth and was quoted as saying, "Oh, what's the use to put it off any longer, I'll kick the box over," and the deed was done. This seems to be a bit more of a fictional account, as this is the only time the execution was recorded in this manner.

After being pronounced dead, his body was cut down and he was placed in the coffin that had shared a ride with him to Diamond Lake. He was transported to Rome City, Indiana, and buried. McDougall is buried in the front row of Northport Cemetery, located on County Road 300 East, between Wolcottville and Rome City.

His headstone remains standing today as one of the only reminders of these dark days in pioneer Indiana. The hanging tree is said to have been cut up and sold for souvenirs years later. Regardless of which account of his execution is accurate, the result was still the same. McDougall was dead and the era of the Blacklegs' reign of terror was all but over. However, even with the death of McDougall, the story and legend of the Blacklegs legacy continued. There were still other Blacklegs roaming northeast Indiana. These eventually fled, were captured, or took the gift given to them and became law-abiding citizens.

Were the Regulators wrong for hanging McDougall? Perhaps there were other, more hardened, criminals behind Blackleg activities, but that fault cannot be found with the Regulators. Although not authorized by law, they acted upon testimony provided by a U.S. Marshal who confirmed that McDougall had in fact committed murder. It is easy for history to be critical of Regulators for

Headstone of Gregor McDougall (spelled incorrectly as McGregor McDougle) located in Northport Cemetery between Rome City and Wolcottville, Indiana. Questions remain if his body was exhumed and removed to his hometown in Canada.

carrying the law too far, but did they have any other choice? If they were to take the chance of holding McDougall in jail, would he have stayed long enough for a court trial? The Regulators had already dealt with numerous escapes from jails all over the region. They had already been victims of retaliation, some of their own barns burned to the ground. How would they deal with the escape of a suspected murderer?

The other option would have been to allow McDougall to be returned to Canada to face trial. Who would have been willing to transport McDougall that distance by horseback? The citizens of the region could not even go out at night without the high likelihood of becoming victims themselves. The manpower needed for this long journey across the Midwest would have been unheard of and virtually impossible for the day.

While some may fault the Regulators for taking the law too far or acting beyond the scope of their authority, most will do so under the impression that the criminal justice system of the period was operating in the same capacity as our modern criminal justice system works today. However, one must take into account the reality of the time period in which McDougall lived and died. The problem lies within the lack of a working justice system in that era of history. It begs the question, if the system does not work, is there really any system at all? The corruption of the local justice system was not a chance the citizens of the region were willing to take. Although McDougall may have served as a scapegoat, the method was very effective.

14. BLACKLEGS DISBANDMENT

After McDougall's execution, as well as other syndicate members throughout the Midwest, the writing was on the wall for any current Blacklegs or anyone considering a similar lifestyle. An example had been made of McDougall by the Regulators and the message was clear: The people of northeast Indiana would no longer idly stand by and watch their belongings disappear. By February of 1858, over fifty arrests had been made by Regulators through Noble and Lagrange Counties in Indiana. The prisoners faced local trials in the county court, or were taken into custody by the U.S. Marshal Service. It was the first recorded overcrowding of the jails in the area of Elkhart, Noble, and Lagrange counties. The number of inmates caused a backlog in the courts. McDougall appears to be the only man executed in Indiana, and possibly the last amongst all of the syndicate.

Regulators in Northest Indiana soon began going after everyone. In Adams County, Indiana, Sheriff Alexander Fleming had long since left office by the time Regulator arrests started in 1858. Fleming was now a Blackleg himself and put up a significant fight when Regulators arrived at his house to affect an arrest. During the fight he severely wounded those who attempted to bring the former sheriff to justice. By January 30, 1858, the Regulators had decided to hang Fleming, but his life was eventually spared.

Indiana Blackleg Miles Payne has perhaps the most interesting story. He was arrested with McDougall by James McConnell and associates in January of 1858. The History of the Regulators identifies Payne as the "Notorious Traitor." Upon his arrest by Regulators, he was perhaps the most cooperative. Payne admitted during his interrogation that he had involved himself in Blackleg activities for about two years, stealing thirty-six horses as well as being involved in the counterfeit business. He became a detective for the Regulators and began arresting his associates. He revealed another connection to Black Rock, Wisconsin, where an additional Blackleg outfit had been operating. After assisting in the arrests of numerous Blacklegs who were turned over to the U.S. Marshals, Payne pulled a disappearing act.

By October of 1858, Payne expressed his reluctance to testify against his friends Perry Randolph and George Ulmer. He disappeared before any judgment could be made against him and was never heard from again. Regulators described him as being approximately twenty-five years old at the time he disappeared in 1858. It is clear through Mott's History of the Regulators that the men despised Payne for having disappeared. By 1878 Payne was working as a foreman at the Stave, Hoop and Barrel Factory in Clermont, Iowa. He was married with ten children and had held the offices of Constable and City Marshal.

The Regulators were turned on to Blackleg Malcom Burnham by the man from whom Burnham bought his property. The men were familiar with Burnham, as he had once pledged to be a Regulator. When Burnham had first arrived in Indiana, he paid cash to an old farmer for some property to build a house. The old farmer later found out that half of the money was counterfeit. Upon his arrest,

Burnham was found to be in possession of a tub full of counterfeit coins.

After being arrested, Burnham faced Regulator-style interrogation. A rope was placed around his neck and he was hung from a rafter until he confessed. Burnham couldn't talk fast enough, his neck still burning from the rope. It was Burnham who accused McDougall of being a ringleader (which was later found to be incorrect). He also accused McDougall of assaulting and robbing the old Scotsman. After he was finished relaying his life of crime, the Regulators had to decide his fate. Some voted in favor of execution, while others voted to spare his life and turn him over to the proper authorities. In the end, the Regulators had a split vote on the decision to execute.

The Regulators could not make a decision, so the punishment phase of the trial was taken to the streets. Arguments broke out as to how Burnham should be punished. Citizens fell to their knees and prayed while speeches were given and the arguments were made. Eventually, the citizens decided on Burnham's fate by popular vote. Those in favor of Burnham's execution were sent to one side of the street, while those opposed were asked to stand on the other side. Luckily for Burnham, there was more room on the side of the street with those in favor of his execution. His life had been spared. Burnham was then sent to the jail at Goshen, Indiana.

The Regulators determined that Burnham had settled in Noble County from Michigan. It was only after Burnham was taken into custody that Regulators learned he fled Michigan to avoid criminal charges. A letter was sent to the Regulators that stated the following:

"Gentlemen: I learn by the public prints that you have succeeded in breaking up a gang of thieves
and robbers who have infested your county and those adjoining. I live at Bell River, St. Clair
County, State of Michigan. All that separates us from the scene of McDougall's former exploits
is the St. Clair River which is about one mile wide. We have for a number of years been troubled
more or less by villains committing their depredations, and crossing back and forth over the river as
it became necessary to escape justice. McDougall has been from here a number of years. A man
by the name of Burnham left here about two years ago. There was at that time an organized band
on both sides of the river, which we have succeeded in breaking up, and some of them are now in
States Prison. This Burnham made his escape and probably took the dies with him. He is about
thirty-five or thirty-eight years old, five feet nine inches high, spare face and brown hair."

Burnham once again found himself in trouble, and this time he would not
escape. He was taken by U.S. Marshals to Indianapolis, where he was indicted on
federal charges in December of 1858. On the same day Burnham was indicted,
Joseph Latta (presumably related to William Latta) of Noble County was in the
same courtroom. No indictment was found against Joseph Latta and the judge
ordered his discharge by the U.S. Marshal from custody. Burnham was indicted on
charges of making counterfeit coin. He was found guilty by Judge Elisha
Huntington in the United States District Court of Indiana. He was fined one dollar
and sentenced to two years of hard labor in the State Prison of Indiana[12].
Regulators from Noble County were reportedly at Burnham's trial, including James

---

[12] Federal prisons were not established until 1891 when Congress passed the "Three Prisons
Act."

McConnell, who had headed up the first arrests. The Prosecutor in the case against Burnham was Daniel Vorhees. After serving as a Federal Prosecutor, Vorhees became a U.S. Senator representing Indiana, where he staunchly fought against the United States' involvement in the Civil War. By all accounts, Burnham took advantage of the gift of life given to him by his fellow citizens, who spared his life by one vote. After his release from prison he returned to Noble County as a farmer. He and his wife Polly (Billings) Burnham eventually moved out to White Cloud, Missouri, where he lived the remainder of his life.

Perry Randolph and George T. Ulmer fled Indiana immediately following the arrests of McDougall and other Blacklegs. Randolph was charged with stealing twelve pairs of gloves from a dry goods store. Ulmer was facing charges of stealing horses from Asa Crape and William Jones, as well as personal goods from Ralph Selby. Both men were still on the run at the time the charges were filed by Special Prosecuting Attorney Robert Parrott. Before leaving, Ulmer confided to a close friend that a mob was coming to take him and feared for his life.

Regulator John Mitchell from Noble County, Indiana

(not in copyright)

The Sheriff of Lagrange County hired Cyrus P. (C.P) Bradley of Chicago and paid him $500 for the capture of these two fugitives. It seems almost impossible that, lacking any modern forms of communication, these fugitives could be tracked so efficiently. Bradley made his first stop in Louisville, Kentucky, but that stop was unproductive. He went up the Ohio River and found the men previously registered at a hotel near Cincinnati, Ohio, but they had since fled. Bradley paid an unannounced visit to Edward Shipley Nevers, a notorious counterfeiter who lived just outside of Cincinnati. Judging by the means in which previous confessions were gained from Blacklegs in Indiana, Nevers decided that sharing information

Vintage ad for the printing company owned by blackleg Edward Nevers

voluntarily was much easier.

Bradley immediately headed to Pittsburgh, Pennsylvania, hot on the trail of the fugitives. Once arriving, Bradley was assisted by Robert Hague, the first chief of police for the City of Pittsburgh. He first laid eyes on the outlaws in Pittsburgh where he spotted Randolph at the Red Lion Hotel. It was familiar territory for Randolph, who was arrested there with William Latta in 1853 for possessing over one thousand counterfeit two-dollar bills. Suspecting that Randolph was traveling with Ulmer, Bradley held off on Randolph's capture and tracked the fugitives to the Old Stone House in Butler County, Pennsylvania.

The Old Stone House was more than just your average hotel and stagecoach stop. It was operated by Julius Holliday and had the reputation as a haven for counterfeit and other thieves. Not surprisingly, Holliday originated from none other than Summit County, Ohio, home of the James Brown Gang. Holliday fled shortly after Brown's arrest and made a new home in Butler, Pennsylvania. It would have been an obvious location for Blacklegs to be hiding.

The Blacklegs were followed to West Greenville in Mercer County, Pennsylvania. Before the capture could be made, their work was complicated by a sick horse. Luckily, they were able to use a fresh team of horses to catch up with both men in Warren, Ohio. In hot pursuit of the fugitives, described by Mott as going ten miles an hour, they finally caught up with Randolph in Newton Falls, Ohio. He was quickly captured and placed in the wagon. Bradley wanted to wait until both men were together to make the arrest, but it didn't happen that way. Hague had to double back to Warren and quickly take Ulmer into custody. Ulmer

161

had been traveling under an alias name of Colonel Foster, and Randolph under the name J.E. Eddie.

The prisoners were taken back to Lagrange County by wagon. Upon entering the small village of South Milford, Indiana, Bradley and his prisoners were met by a parade of Regulators. Undoubtedly this unnerved the prisoners, who had already learned of McDougall's fate. Some residents wanted the fugitives to be turned over to the Blacklegs. Others suspected the Regulators would hang these men without

Warrant for the arrest of George Randolph, brother to Perry Randolph, issued by the Circuit Court of Lagrange County. (courtesy of Lagrange County GIS)

Warrant for the arrest of Perry Randolph and George Ulmer, sent to the Sheriff of DeKalb County, Indiana from the Circuit Court of Lagrange, Indiana. (courtesy of Lagrange County GIS)

the benefit of a trial, and demanded they be turned over to the sheriff.

According to author Howard Troyer, the scene quickly turned violent. Fistfights broke out in the street and heated arguments continued. Eventually gunfire erupted amongst the crowd. Luckily most of the shots were in the air, but one of them hit a local resident in the arm, causing severe injuries. Cooler heads finally prevailed. On July 11, 1858, seven months after they fled northeast Indiana, both men were turned over to the custody of Lagrange County Sheriff Cummings.

Randolph was indicted in Lagrange County and later extradited to Dekalb

County, Indiana. He was put on trial, where his former Blackleg associate John

"Flying Dutchman" Wilson testified against him. The strongest case presented by

the state was on a burglary charge. He was convicted of stealing twelve pairs of

gloves from a dry goods store in the small town of Ontario in Lagrange County

and sentenced to serve two years in the penitentiary. Ulmer was charged with

counterfeiting and theft. He was also found guilty and given a seven-year sentence.

George Randolph, brother of Perry Randolph, was charged in the Lagrange

Circuit Court for receiving stolen goods after being found in possession of

property belonging to William Selby. George Randolph had also fled the state

when the Regulators began arresting Blacklegs, but was later captured. Presumably

he did not serve a very long sentence.

As for the man who apprehended these criminals, his story has a happier

ending. Perhaps due to his ability to track down the fugitives of the day, C.P.

Bradley's career advanced considerably upon his return to Chicago. He served two

*Cyrus P. (C.P) Bradley, fugitive
hunter and later named first
chief of police in Chicago,
Illinois (not in copyright)*

ST. LOUIS, 6th.

GREAT GREENBACK COUNTERFEITING.

A special despatch to the Republican from Kansas City, says large quantities of counterfeit greenbacks have been discovered afloat in the southwest counties of Kansas. Suspicions pointing to Perry Randolph, an old farmer, living near White Pigeon, Michigan, as being the principal vender of the stuff, a U. S. detective, assuming the name of Johnsen of Texas, wrote to Randolph for $16,000, agreeing to pay $2,000 therefor. Randolph replied that he would bring the amount to Kansas. He arrived Wednesday last, and was met by the detective who arrested him. He confessed his guilt and in default of $10,000 bail, was committed to jail to await trial.

Arrest of Perry Randolph, from the Lewiston Evening Journal, December 7, 1868 (not in copyright)

terms as sheriff in Cook County, Illinois. Most notably, he was eventually named the first chief of police for the City of Chicago.

After serving his sentence, Randolph returned to his life as a farmer in Lagrange. By 1870, Randolph relocated to nearby Goshen in Elkhart County and later up to St. Joseph County, Michigan. He was not able to stay out of trouble completely, however. Even as late as 1868, Randolph was still having an occasional brush with the law.

Described by the *Syracuse Daily Journal* as an "old farmer" from White Pigeon, Randolph was arrested in Kansas City that year for passing counterfeit money. He remained behind bars in Missouri until February of the following year. After his sentence was complete he was once again a free man. Randolph died on April 10, 1879, and is buried in Florence Township, St. Joseph County, Michigan. Ulmer, one of the pioneers of Lagrange and Noble County, returned home and lived the remainder of his life in Pretty Prairie, Lagrange County. There is no indication Ulmer ever returned to his former ways of thieving and counterfeiting. He died December 2, 1891, near Wolcottville, Indiana. In St. Joseph County, Michigan, William Latta was back into trouble by 1857. Latta had brought up his son Napoleon B. Latta learning the family counterfeiting trade, and soon they were both brought up on counterfeiting charges. William "Old Man" Latta and his son Napoleon put up the hotel and tavern as bond, along with all of their encompassing land. William fled the area to Iowa, but Napoleon made one

Regulator Charles Cochran, from the History of Lagrange County. (not in copyright)

last-ditch effort to save himself and the family business. He managed to convince the Prosecutor that he was actually working undercover for one of Pinkerton's detectives. Though it bought him a little time, it wasn't long before even Napoleon was smart enough to see the writing on the wall. He too fled, but chose Monroe, Wisconsin, as his new home. The hotel and tavern were forfeited to the county, who turned the building into a home for the poor. For Napoleon, moving to a new city did not mean starting over. By 1871, Napoleon Latta was back in prison, serving a ten-year sentence after being found with stolen U.S. Treasury printing plates.

After William Latta wore out his welcome in Indiana and Michigan, he escaped to Iowa. His escape was made soon after the arrests of the first few Blacklegs. Although Latta escaped from the Regulators, it does not appear that he could remain crime-free. He was arrested in 1859 in Davenport, Iowa, on counterfeiting charges. By June of 1860 he was convicted and serving time in the Iowa Penitentiary. Perhaps he learned from the error of his ways, or perhaps he just got too old to commit crimes after his release from prison. Latta later moved to Wisconsin, where he lived the remainder of his life as a farmer. There is no evidence that authorities ever worked to have him returned to Indiana.

William "Bill" Hill upheld his reputation for being a hardened and violent criminal. After a search warrant was served at Hill's residence, an argument broke out that resulted in Hill being shot in the thigh. He soon disappeared before any charges could be brought upon him. Bradley and another detective identified as C.E. Smith tracked Hill to Iowa, near the Missouri line, where he was living on a large farm. He had previously vowed that he would never be taken alive, but after a fierce fight with C.P. Bradley that lasted an estimated fifteen minutes, Hill was taken into custody and returned to Indiana. He was returned to Indiana after Randolph and Ulmer had already been brought to justice. Hill was taken to the Noble County Jail. Either through Blackleg associates or by his own craftiness, Hill escaped from the Noble County Jail along with "Flying Dutchman" Wilson in March of 1858 and was never heard from again. Some claim that Hill only escaped out of fear of hanging like McDougall. Hill may have been better off facing the justice system, as the political connections with this organized crime outfit were strong.

Out in Nauvoo, Illinois, local residents still associated all of the Blackleg crimes with the local Mormons. A vigilante mob had already taken the life of Mormon founder Joseph Smith, but that did not satisfy the vigilantes. A list of Mormon-related criminals was publicly posted and anti-Mormons ran for office on that very platform. Amongst the identified accused in the History of Lee County were Jeremiah Plumb, Mark Childs, E.C. Richardson, Nathaniel Eames, William Hickman, Philander Avery, Levi Wickeron, Jonathan Barlow, Jefferson Bradley, Alvin Sanford, Jedidiah Owens, Samuel Musick, Nelson Benton, Robert Owen, Samuel Avery, Sylvester Jackson, and Ethan Pettit. The anti-Mormon ticket won by a landslide and all able-bodied Mormons were expelled from Lee County. The Mormon history sees this incident in a different light and calls it an "exile." However, the Mormon struggle in Nauvoo is enough for a book in itself.

Though there were some former Mormons involved in Blackleg activity, the anti-Mormon movement seems to be without just cause. Besides ex-communicating several Blacklegs, Mormon leaders appear to have been victimized like many others in the same community. The advice given by Brigham Young and William Smith seems more than reasonable, asking the accused to turn themselves in to the proper authorities. Regardless, the Mormons knew better than to stay. Brigham Young came to an agreement with the Governor of Illinois and was living in Utah as of 1847.

There are rumors throughout the legacy of the Blacklegs of these high level political connections. More than one accusation was leveled in historical books that Blacklegs had connections to the highest levels of government. It has already been established that Blacklegs had their hands in the pockets of judges, sheriffs, and other local officials. But exactly how high were the Blacklegs' connections?

After his arrest in Summit County, Ohio, James Brown was confined to the Ohio State Penitentiary. Citing exemplary behavior while working at the prison medical unit, Brown was given a full pardon by Zachary Taylor, twelfth President of the United States. In February of 1860, Perry Randolph and George Ulmer were both pardoned by governor Ashbel Parsons Willard of Indiana. Both men served less than two years of their seven-year sentence. Willard provided no explanation to the public. The community was rightfully outraged. Out in Iowa, William Latta served less than one year of his sentence before being granted a full pardon by the governor, Samuel J. Kirkwood. Just like Willard, Kirkwood would offer no explanation for this decision. Kirkwood would later serve as U.S. Senator and Secretary for the Department of Interior under President Garfield.

McDougall mentioned in his own confession that his associate Sherman

Mallet was pardoned out of prison. The reach of their political connections may

have gone into Canada as well, as Mallet never served his full sentence. Gregor

McDougall's older brother Miles was pardoned out of the penitentiary in Kingston,

Ontario, in 1868. It does not appear that anyone received any significant

punishment, other than those who were lynched by Regulators. Perhaps frontier

justice and a trial before "Judge Lynch," as it was referred to, was in fact the only

true justice that could be found at the time.

Zachary Taylor, 12th President of the United States, who pardoned Jim Brown from prison. (photo from the Library of Congress Digital Image Collection, not in copyright)

DAWSON'S DAILY TIMES.

FORT WAYNE,
FRIDAY EVENING, FEB. 24, 1860.

AN EXPOSITION.

The Pardon of Perry Randolph!
WHO IS RESPONSIBLE?

Up in Wisconsin, Napoleon Latta received a pardon from President Ulysses S. Grant. Napoleon's pardon seems to be a little more justified more than the rest. His wife had been working with the Secret Service to identify additional counterfeiters in exchange for her husband's release. He stayed crime-free for the remainder of his life.

There is really no way to determine the true extent of political connections made by the Blacklegs. Were any of these politicians on the payrolls of Blacklegs, or is this all a mere coincidence? It certainly is suspicious that so many pardons were granted after such short terms of their sentences were served. Rumors have circulated that Blacklegs would contribute large amounts of money (all counterfeit, of course) to the campaign funds of politicians. The truth may never be known.

Though the stealing of horses remained steady for many decades afterward, most of the organized activity seems to have slowed by the 1860's. Of course counterfeiting has been a continual problem carried even to the present day, but

171

the widespread distribution of standard U.S. currency made this activity much more difficult. The invention of the telegraph and other technology of that era also put a damper on the Blacklegs' ability to continue with their operations. The final nail in the Blacklegs' coffin was the election of President Abraham Lincoln and the start of the American Civil War.

15. MCDOUGALL MURDER CONTROVERSY

As previously stated, one of the main goals of this book is to examine all the facts and try to set the record of history straight. While this can sometimes be very difficult considering the age of some records, a plethora of sources with different portrayals of events, and the lack of verifiable facts, the goal should always remain the same. In this case, a lack of information may be the best proof. Almost every local history book in northeast Indiana reports that McDougall was executed after being found guilty of two murders which occurred in Canada.

McDougall's trial before the Central Committee consisted of an examination of all the facts and allegations against McDougall. The testimony included that of Deputy U.S. Marshal Halstead. Deputy Halstead testified that he had been to Canada personally and learned that McDougall was wanted for the murder of the jailor's wife and one other murder, which took place during a robbery. The case was rather simple. Who else would provide more reliable testimony than a Deputy U.S. Marshal? Regulators had no reason to doubt the testimony of the Deputy Marshal.

The accusations of murder against McDougall have been longstanding. The History of Whitley County, Indiana by Kaler and Maring reports, "On January 16, 1858, a demonstration was made in Kendallville by the Regulators of the surrounding country. The next day, January 17th, active hostility began by the arrest of a dozen or more of the most notorious blacklegs. This was in a few days followed by the hanging of Gregory McDougall, **a triple murderer** and all around criminal." There is no doubt McDougall was an all-around outlaw and criminal. But was he actually a murderer?

Mott's account of the Regulators' activities indicates that a Deputy U.S. Marshal from Michigan testified under oath that McDougall was wanted for jailbreak and murder. The murder apparently happened when McDougall broke his brother Miles out of jail in Chatham, Ontario, Canada.

The Deputy U.S. Marshal reportedly made two trips to Canada to investigate the murder of the person McDougall had already confessed to robbing. That person was the wife of the jailor who maintained the lockup where Miles McDougall was confined. The second murder McDougall was accused of committing was that of Alexander McCoy. From McDougall's confession, he claimed McCoy was not even hurt.

If you will recall, one of the main problems that contributed to the Blacklegs' success was a lack of trained law enforcement. There were very few Deputy U.S. Marshals for the entire state. There was also a very high turnover rate, with most of the Deputy Marshals appointed serving less than a year. A Deputy U.S. Marshal's appointment was not a career back then; it was generally almost a side job for some, as they were underpaid and given very few resources. Gathering information back then was not as easy as picking up a phone. It required weeks and months of travel. Information was gathered from others under identical circumstances, under-trained and inexperienced law enforcers who operated under very few standards.

It was because of the crimes of which McDougall was accused, Mott claims, that the Regulators made the decision to execute. Numerous people have investigated the accusations against McDougall, that he killed the jailor's wife and McCoy. Attorney and historian John Martin Smith, retired schoolteacher and historian Roy McGregor, historian J. Thomas Kerr from the Toronto area, genealogist Barbara Thornton, and others (besides this author) have all come to the conclusion that the murders never happened. There is evidence of a jailbreak in Canada, which in fact led to several arrests. However, none of those accused in this incident were ever charged with murder or being an accessory to a murder. Further, there is nothing in local history records in the Wallaceburg or Chatham area that ever recorded the murder of a jailor's wife, or the murder of a man named McCoy. Murders of any kind were major news stories back in the 1850's. Certainly the murder of a jailor's wife would have been documented in some local history accounts. The murder of John Nelles by the Townsend Gang is well documented and recorded in newspapers throughout history up to the present day. There is a complete absence of any documentation for murder in which McDougall was supposedly involved.

Oddly enough, during the interviews conducted by A.M. Groves for his 1910 article, Regulator Charles Inks claims the murders were of a husband and wife near Wolf Lake, Indiana, which is right in Noble County. Certainly if McDougall had involved himself in the murders of anyone in Noble County, Indiana, M.H. Mott would have documented these facts when discussing the case built against

175

McDougall. It would have been a source of pride for the Regulators to capture someone who committed murder in their own back yard, and they would have certainly wanted to take the credit for bringing a murderer to justice. Instead, Mott only detailed murders that occurred up in Canada and mentions nothing of any such crime in Indiana.

The local newspaper in Newmarket, Ontario, Canada published a similar story following McDougall's execution. Their account of McDougall also accuses him of committing murder in Indiana, with no mention of Canada. If there was a murder in Canada, it would have certainly been mentioned in a newspaper from that same area. If there was in fact a reward issued for the arrest of McDougall, why wasn't this included in the article as well?

There is also a lack of documented facts surrounding the murders from the Regulators themselves. Their book does not mention a victim's name, location, or any specific information other than the claim that murders were committed. The Regulators did publish a letter received from F.C. Chamberlain, the Postmaster in Rushville, New York. He sent the following letter, which was reprinted in Mott's History of the Regulators:

Rushville, NY

Mar. 22, 1858

Mr. Postmaster,

As I have just read an account of the execution and confession of Gregory McDougall,

at your place on the 26th of January last, and (has- as ?) many have no confidence in

such confessions made at such times and under such circumstances, I thought I would

write and let you know that all those acts, except the horse stealing, which he says

transpired in this country are true. His statement in reference to the store which was

broken in Chemung County is also true, and the Baker whom he mentions is a man

living in Pen Yan, as he says. I have showed the confession to the sheriff of our county,

and he says he is acquainted with the said Baker, Joseph Howard and several other

hard cases he mentions. I see by the papers you are doing good work. I write that you

may know that many of the statements made in said confession, in reference to his acts

in this country are true.

F. C. Chamberlain, P.M.

Notice the letter from the postmaster mentions nothing of bringing a
murderer to justice. It says the acts in his confession are true; however, there is
nothing to say what was communicated to the postmaster. In his confession,
McDougall clearly denied committing murders. The confession mentions a store
was broken into, so it would be reasonable that if a murder was committed there
would be some mention of it in this letter. It is just another piece to a complicated

puzzle that raises doubt upon the notion that McDougall was guilty of murder.

The best evidence favoring McDougall's innocence on the charge of murder comes from Goodspeed's book written in 1882. A mere twenty-four years after McDougall's execution, Goodspeed confirms that the Regulators knew there was not a murder case against McDougall. Having first-hand knowledge based upon those involved still being alive, Goodspeed wrote that the Regulators only had enough evidence to charge McDougall with murder. The Regulators recommended the death sentence as a result of the charges. Further, Goodspeed alleges the Regulators only hung McDougall because he was a hardened criminal, not because any of the Regulators actually thought McDougall was in fact a murderer. The citizens could not handle the activities of the Blacklegs any longer, and executing McDougall was viewed as the only option to stop the Blacklegs from terrorizing the community further. As a side note, Goodspeed mentions that Deputy Marshal Halstead was threatened with lynching after returning to Ligonier following McDougall's execution. Curiously enough, Mott's History of the Regulators mentions nothing about the doubt raised on the murders pinned on McDougall. Perhaps the feelings of guilt were still too fresh, or perhaps they had not yet discovered McDougall was innocent of the murder charge.

It is possible the accusations made against McDougall are a case of mistaken identity. In 1846, a Lorne McDougall, Gregor's brother, was sentenced to eight years in the Kingston Pen for horse stealing and intent to murder. Perhaps it was a case of miscommunication during a time when communication was very difficult. It is also possible that McDougall's association with Townsend became twisted over the course of time. The Deputy Marshal reported that McDougall was wanted for murder. Perhaps this was confused with McDougall being an accomplice of Townsend, who was in fact still wanted for murder up in Canada. McDougall was accused of robbing a man who fell on the ice and died. One of Townsend's accomplices who robbed a man was shot on the ice and later died. This is about as close as any historical records can connect McDougall to a murder.

Modern day references in Canada make no mention of any murder. In 2011, an article appeared in a Chatham publication outlining the details surrounding the Wallaceburg-born man Gregor McDougall and how he was lynched by an angry mob. The story relays how McDougall tried to unsuccessfully break his brother out of jail and was soon sought by authorities. The article makes no mention of any murder during the jailbreak, which would certainly be notable for any historical account of such an incident.

The murder accusations may also have come from a Blackleg such as Miles Payne, who was working hard to absolve himself of any charges. If a hardened criminal can turn state's evidence and make someone else look guiltier, the heat can be turned on someone else. Perhaps this was the case with McDougall, and he was framed by members of his own gang.

There were undoubtedly feelings of guilt on the part of those involved in the McDougall execution. It goes beyond the threats made to lynch the Deputy U.S. Marshal, who was subsequently run out of town with warnings to never return. In Troyer's book Salt and Savor, he mentions that one Regulator committed suicide after being consumed with guilt, presumably over involvement in the execution of

179

McDougall.

Although he was a criminal, it should be glaringly obvious after reading the punishment received by other members of the syndicate that McDougall's execution was not justified in the eyes of history. In the command structure of organized crime, McDougall would have been on the lowest level. Other members such as Sile Doty or William Latta had decades of history with the Blacklegs. McDougall was a newly married man in his 20's with a young child. Seeing how none of the other members of the outfit spent more than a year or two in jail, the idea of McDougall paying for his crimes with his life seems completely unjustifiable.

Even today, mentions in some modern historical books in the Indiana area still reference McDougall as being a murderer. Although the accusations seem to be corrected within the years immediately following his execution, there has been a shift in the opposite direction ever since. Hopefully through this book and the documentation provided by others, history will eventually be reported correctly.

16. AFTERMATH

The era of the Blacklegs is one of the violent periods in American history, which has been all but forgotten. It is also rarely recognized as the first organized crime in American history. Interestingly, it was not law enforcement, the courts, technology, or any branch of the government responsible for quashing this band of outlaws. As has been recounted in this story, it was the pioneers and average citizens of the day who found justice when the system failed, even though their actions were unjustified on more than one occasion.

The Blacklegs and their associates stole countless horses. They murdered dozens of innocent men and printed hundreds of thousands (or more) in counterfeit money. Between 1846 and the beginning of the Civil War, over forty-five people were lynched in Iowa alone. The overwhelming majority were horse thieves and counterfeiters, likely tied to the organized crime syndicate. Countless others were executed after being convicted and sentenced to death in established courts.

There are indications from Iowa that in addition to the lynchings, other Regulator activity soon got out of hand. There are several reports of Regulator-style intimidation acts toward anyone who dared to cross them. In one case, the local assessor placed higher property values on some local property causing an increase in taxes. Regardless of whether this was a mistake or intentional, he was soon visited by a band of Regulators who ordered him to leave town or face death. A local surveyor left town under similar circumstances, after receiving the same warning from Regulators.

Anyone remotely connected with the Blacklegs was under immediate suspicion by the Regulators and the community. Every outlaw arrested faced full questioning by Regulator companies to see what intelligence could be gained. In Indiana, over a dozen people were lynched at the hands of Regulator-style companies by 1869, the majority being in southern Indiana.[13] Dr. Sutton, a Blackleg from Lagrange County, Indiana, decided he would not wait to suffer the wrath of the Regulators. Rather than face arrest, Sutton took his own life with the powerful opiate drug Laudanum shortly after McDougall was arrested.

Those Blacklegs not charged were questioned, gave full confessions, and were released to return home with their lives spared. Many of them went on to live peaceful lives as law-abiding citizens. Some even went on to serve as constables or held other public offices serving their community. While this may sound unusual, remember that even famous lawman Wyatt Earp was once a horse thief. It was a different kind of forgiveness, which is not afforded to criminals today. When the 1860's rolled around, some of the Blacklegs were the first in line to enlist in the Civil War.

McDougall may have pulled his final escape act, but not on his own accord. There are two historical reports that family members dug up McDougall and

---

[13] At least six members of the Reno gang were lynched in southern Indiana in 1868 by the Jackson County Vigilance Committee in two different incidents.

removed his body back to Canada where he was buried at an undisclosed location. Even if his remains may have been removed, his gravestone remains standing today in Northport Cemetery, between Rome City and Wolcottville. It is just a short distance from the area formerly known as Tamarack, which was once headquarters for Blackleg activities.

Margaret McDougall, the widow of Gregor, filed a lawsuit against the Regulators responsible for her husband's death. The case was filed in the U.S. District Court but a settlement was reached before the case ever went to trial. There are estimates the settlement ranged from $300 - $10,000, though she initially sued for $25,000. There are stories that Margaret received financial support from undisclosed sources for years following the hanging of her husband. There are two stories that have been told regarding this financial support. One hints that sympathetic Blacklegs provided Margaret with money to survive, giving her profits from their own misdoings. Other stories relay that Regulators suffering from the guilt of hanging a man, innocent of the murders of which he was accused, gave Margaret money as a way of soothing their own consciences.

McDougall's widow moved back to the area of Wallaceburg, Canada and married Gregor McDougall's cousin John McGregor. With her new husband she had five children: Chester, John, Vada, William, and Theresa. Gregor and Margaret's only child, daughter Ida McDougall, married James Cross on October 8,

I have just examined the docket of the District
Court of the United States for Indiana, and find
that the matter to which I referred some days
ago in your columns, that Margaret McDougal
has not as yet sued the parties who hung her
husband, Gregor McDougal, at Diamond Lake in
Noble county, in January, 1858, but that on the
19th of January last she, administratrix of Gregor McDougal, by her attorney, John R. Coffroth of
Huntington, filed a *precipe* with the clerk of that
court, claiming damages in the sum of $25,000
of Harrison Wood, Charles T. Wheeler, Jerome
Sweet, Gilbert Sherman, J. E. Braden, and
Leonard Barber of Noble county, and Jas. Fuller
of Allen county; and that *for the want of bond
for cost*, the writ has not been issued. Why this
unholy proceeding? There is some person who
moves like a thief in the night, trying to harrass
those to whom the whole of Northern Indiana are
indebted for a great good. The matter will however, I think, end where it is.

*Report on the lawsuit filed by the widow of Gregor McDougall. (not
in copyright)*

1873, in Gregor's hometown of Wallaceburg and lived the rest of her life in

Detroit, Michigan. McDougall's widow Margaret died on May 11, 1911. Crime did

not come to a complete halt following arrests by the Regulators. In 1859, the

Noble County Courthouse in Albion, Indiana, was burned to the ground. The

investigation revealed arson was the most likely cause. While there were no direct

accusations that Blacklegs were involved, it certainly did happen at a most suspicious time in the region's history when all efforts were being made to disband this criminal organization.

There are two reports of the demise of William 'Bill' Hill, suspected of being the fugitive William Townsend. Although one tale reports Hill lived the life of a farmer in rural Missouri, another is a little more violent. The Lagrange Standard published a story in 1876 that reported Hill had relocated to Arkansas. Continuing the life of an outlaw, Hill announced himself as a Doctor and began practicing medicine. The Civil War broke out, but Hill was able to maintain friendships with the Confederates, even though he was from the north. Eventually the Union Army made their way to Hill's hometown, where he found himself in a most awkward position.

Through his conniving ways, Hill gained the confidence of a local army captain from the Union side. Hill conspired with the army captain to poison Confederates through tainted medicine. Apparently the local Confederates heard of this sinister plan and did not take too kindly to Hill's efforts. Hill was captured, beaten to death, and had his body shredded by an angry mob.

If Hill was actually Townsend as suspected, this explains why nothing more was ever heard of Townsend or Hill. It is also fits with the various characterizations of Townsend, which describe him as a good actor; he was a good enough actor to convince others that he was actually a physician. Unfortunately, his final act was not so pleasant.

INDIANA "REGULATORS."—We learn from the Indianapolis *Journal*, that the Southern portion of Indiana seems to be constantly infested with thieves, counterfeiters, and other scoundrels, who are either protected or actively assisted by certain residents, and thus enabled to escape the slow moving justice of law. So great have the depredations of these characters become, that the citizens have felt driven to the extremity of organizing a band of "Regulators," after the manner in Noble County. The murder and attempted robbery of an old German in Greene County, the circulation of unusual quantities of counterfeit money, and the presence of several citizens of much worse than suspicious reputations, appear to have been the impelling causes of the movement, aggravating a long-slumbering fear and dislike of the rascally citizens in question. A meeting of the citizens of two townships was held on the 2d inst., when it was resolved that STEPHEN SCAGGS, JOSEPH ELLIS, GEORGE BURTON, WM. FIELDS and JOSEPH SMITH "leave the State of Indiana" on short notice, and that "WM. GROVE immediately close up his grocery," and quit selling liquor," &c.

Article on the Indiana Regulators, from the New York Times, June 21, 1858 (not in copyright)

Following the hanging of McDougall, the threat of Regulator activity was sometimes enough to deter crime, at least in Indiana. One notice published to the citizens of Greene County, Indiana, specifically addressed five local Blacklegs. The ad from the local Regulator company warned five suspected thieves to "leave the State of Indiana on short notice," and further warned a local grocer named William Grove to "immediately close up his grocery and quit selling liquor." Obviously the Regulators felt comfortable these men would heed public warning given to them. The Regulators remained determined to rid the Midwest of all thieves, counterfeiters, and other criminals. By most accounts, their efforts evolved from quasi-law enforcement into somewhat of a witch-hunt. Their zealous ways soon turned into problems for the Regulators themselves.

The first sign of problems for the Regulators was in September 1858, less than a year after McDougall's execution. Local Fort Wayne resident George Palmer had been accused by a Regulator of manufacturing counterfeit money. The accusations appear to be false. Palmer published an open letter in the Fort Wayne Sentinel proclaiming his innocence and challenging the Regulators' actions.

By October 1858, Sheriff Flemming of nearby Allen County, who fought against the Blacklegs, faced his own difficulties while running for re-election. Area residents confused Flemming with the former sheriff of neighboring Adams County, who was an identified Blackleg. This was partially due to the efforts by the other candidate for sheriff who was accused of intentionally promoting the same falsehoods. As a result, Flemming's re-election efforts were spent clearing up any notion in the eyes of the voter that he was the sheriff turned Blackleg or even a sympathizer to the outlaw gang.

Public opinion gradually began to sway against the Regulators, partially due to the hanging of McDougall. Although Regulator activities would continue for several decades, they were monitored with closer scrutiny. In February 1859, a little over one year after the McDougall execution, one Regulator company in Indiana submitted a request for reimbursement through the state for their costs

Fort Wayne Sentinel, printed September 19, 1858 (not in copyright)

tracking down horse thieves. One legislator specifically addressed the "murderous hanging of McDougall," while another referred to Regulators as a "curse to the people" during the debate. There was even some argument about whether the law authorizing the formation of Regulator companies should be repealed.

In March 1861, the Common Pleas Court of Allen County, Indiana found a judgment in favor of accused Blackleg George Culver. After being falsely arrested, Culver sued four local Regulators in civil court for damages. The court found in favor of Culver for $150. According to the 1861 Dawson's Fort Wayne Daily

Times, the judgment was "$150 too much and the people of Allen County ought to pay it, as a very small compensation for the good the Regulators did them." This was an obvious commentary but was still reflective of the support even then lingering for the Regulators.

In the Court of Common Pleas of Allen county a verdict was this day, March 4th, returned for $150 damages, in a case where George Culver sued David Archer, Elbridge Burk, Danl. Foss and J. L. Fuller of Perry township, for trespass. They were regulators and took up Culver, and did the thing decently too, and yet they are thus mulct in damages. The verdict is $150 too much, and the people of Allen county ought to pay it, as a very small compensation for the good the Regulators did them. We always will accord to the Regulators praise, for we know they deserve it bountifully.

Dawson's Fort Wayne Daily Times, March 1861 (not in copyright)

In 1869, the state legislature publicly denounced Regulator companies throughout the state in a joint resolution. The resolution was adopted as follows:

OUTRAGES BY REGULATORS OR VIGILANCE COMMITTEES.

Mr. CARSON offered the following joint resolution [S. 8.]

WHEREAS, The reputation of our beloved State has been seriously injured, since the last session of the General Assembly, in repeated instances, by the execution of prisoners accused of crime by mob violence; and,

WHEREAS, Within that time more than a dozen of persons have thus suffered death at the hands of organized bands of men, not acting under the impulse of momentary passion occasioned by some outrage just discovered, but proceeding with a deliberate determination, that evinced a purpose to permit no law, human or divine, to stand in the way of the accomplishment of their object; and,

WHEREAS, These bold perpetrators of those heinous crimes have thus far escaped detection and punishment; and,

WHEREAS, In the language of our constitution it is especially made the duty of the Governor that "he shall take care that the laws be faithfully executed." Now therefore--

BE IT RESOLVED by the General Assembly of the State of Indiana, That for the purpose of detecting and bringing to punishment the perpetrators of those diabolical crimes and offenses, and also for the purpose of detecting and bringing to merited punishment, all such as may hereafter be guilty of like grave offenses, there be set apart, out of any moneys not otherwise appropriated in the State Treasury, the sum of ten

thousand dollars, to be expended by the Governor, at his discretion, or so much thereof

as he may deem necessary for the purpose contemplated by this preamble and resolution,

which sum shall be drawn by the Governor at such times as he shall require the same.

Provided, That no greater sum shall be drawn at any time than shall be by him

necessarily expended;

Although the days of Blacklegs and Regulators are long over, the debate

behind their activities remains today. There was agreement even amongst the

Regulators that boundaries were overstepped in the case of McDougall. However,

it should not be inferred that the Regulators apologized, or felt the need to

apologize for their hand in McDougall's death. Even those Regulators in Iowa and

Illinois who were charged with crimes resulting from lynching were never

convicted. This is mostly due to the times in which these events took place. Horse

thieves and counterfeiters were destroying communities. The Regulators, who tried

to bring justice back, were the prominent members of the community. It was an

easy choice for most as there was no third option.

Stealing a horse was much more serious than most people realize in today's

society. As of 1817, horse theft was punishable by twenty-five to thirty-nine lashes

for the first offense; the second offense was punishable by death. Therefore,

McDougall's admission of stealing thirty-four horses was certainly enough to earn

the death penalty of the day. The method of obtaining his confession as well as the

trial before the central committee was obviously beyond rightfulness, but it was effective in starting to disband the Regulators nonetheless. With the lack of an

impartial criminal justice system, the Regulators likely had an easy time maintaining

public support for their actions until the memories of the McDougall lynching had

all but faded.

Regulator activity in northeast Indiana continued as late as July 3, 1902.
Printed in the New York Sun. (not in copyright)

The Blacklegs' activities can be viewed in a positive light to some extent. By 1865, Congress had passed an act creating the United States Secret Service to actively investigate financial crimes such as counterfeiting. Although most view the role of the Secret Service as protecting the President and other dignitaries, it was actually created as an enforcement arm to contain the problem of counterfeit currency, which has assisted in stabilizing the nation's economy. The Secret Service did not actually assume the role of protective details until after 1900. The problem of counterfeiting also encouraged the idea of creating a national currency through the United States Treasury.

Early photo of Secret Service Agents, courtesy of the Library of Congress (not in copyright)

Even today, the actions of the Regulators are still in debate. Historical recounts of Regulator activities question their effectiveness, as serious crimes continued in Noble County for decades to follow. Even as recently as 1997, the Valparaiso Law School in Indiana debated Regulator activities and cited the McDougall execution in their discussion of how vigilante law evolved. Undoubtedly, future historians, researchers of law, genealogists, and other interested parties will keep the story of Blacklegs, Regulators, and McDougall alive for the next generation.

There is one final chapter to the Blacklegs legacy and that is the story of lost treasure. As you have read, one of the Blacklegs' chief sources of income was the sale of counterfeit money. The going rate at the time was to sell five dollars in counterfeit for every one dollar of legitimate currency. Many of the Blacklegs saved the legitimate currency and gold for their own use, while using counterfeit for their daily affairs. As banks were not insured (nor the safest place to store valuables), many pioneers of the day, including Blacklegs, kept their money at home. In the case of the Blacklegs, home was not always the safest place either, so there have been a few tales of buried treasure.

The first is involving the murderous Micajah and Wiley Harpe. Several different accounts of buried treasure have been connected with these two men. One report is that the men have a stash of gold coins hidden in a cave above a stream in Henderson County, Kentucky. When Micajah Harpe was killed by the posse tracking him down, he supposedly was in possession of two saddlebags full of silver which have never been recovered. If he in fact had that silver, it would likely be somewhere in the area of Harpe's Head Corner in Kentucky.

On a side note, the treasure left behind by the Harpes brothers, if it does exist, is not the only legend left behind. There are two plays written about the Harpes. The first was in 1942, when Eudora Welty wrote a novel called _Robber Bridegroom_ which was eventually transformed into a Broadway play which ran through the mid 1970's. The play is loosely based upon history and portrays Little Harpe and Big Harpe. The theme of the show is a man trying to win the love of a plantation owner along the Natchez Trail. In the story, Big Harpe is put to death for stealing. Little Harpe then carries around his older brother's severed head in a trunk. Though no longer on Broadway, the play is now performed by theatrical groups and schools across the nation, doubtfully with the knowledge one of the characters was America's first serial killer. The second more recent play is _American Misfit_ by Dan Dietz, which is set to a rock-a-billy theme.

Along the face of the cliff at Cave-in-Rock, there are reportedly other stashes of gold coin left behind by Samuel Mason. With all of the other riverboats and stagecoaches who found themselves on the wrong hand of Blacklegs from that era, there are rumors of another $200,000 hidden around that same area. Confirmed cases of coins and other treasure washing up in that area have occurred in the past, so this story may be more likely than others. Connected with Mason are other caches of gold that are alleged to be near Little Sand Creek in Stack Island, Mississippi. Another $250,000 is said to be buried near Bissell, Mississippi.

Another story of hidden treasure involves the wealth of Sile Doty. The swamps near Fremont, Indiana, which have mostly been drained, was the burial site for some of Doty's loot. Since his death, there was one report of $1,000 found and another of $500. Based upon his own admission of the crimes in which he was involved, it is likely there remains additional buried treasure somewhere in the northeastern part of Steuben County. From Doty's biography, we know that he lived in the property owned by Stimpson near Fremont. There was only one Stimpson family from that era living in Fremont at the time, and that would be Sumner and Joanna Stimpson.

There is at least one estimate that Doty has over $250,000 in the swamps around Fremont, which would likely be near the old Stimpson property. That dollar figure was based upon the value when it was hidden. If it is ever discovered, it would be now be worth millions. The claim of this missing loot was reported in the now defunct Treasure Magazine. It was based on interviews done with the McElroy family who became friends with Sile Doty before his death.

The article, written by Maurice Kildare, portrays Doty as an old miser and loner who hid money all around the local swamps in an effort to keep it safe from his fellow thieves. But, there are some notable errors in the article, including an erroneous date of death for Doty. The article claims he recovered from an attack in 1878, when he was known to have died two years prior. The article by Kildare makes a most interesting claim that Doty was once a member of the Jesse James Gang. This is a rumor that has surfaced in the past so it may have some level of truth, but no smoking gun has ever been found.

Further evidence Doty may have some hidden money can be found in the connection made in this article with a man named George Downing. Downing was one of four brothers, including one named William Downing. This is the same

William Downing who was once a member of the Sam Bass Outlaw Gang. There are claims George and William Downing had countless money of their own buried in the area between Clear Lake and Fremont, Indiana, where they lived.

The millions Doty had hidden is comparable to the money which may have been hidden by the family of former counterfeiter Jim Brown. Old Sheriff Samuel Lane from Summit County, Ohio may have thought when the California Gold Rush broke out he would find a legal way to make himself rich after watching the Browns make their fortune through printing fake money. He packed up and headed west, leaving his family behind.

While in Sacramento, California, Lane ran into none other than Dan Brown Jr., son of counterfeiter Dan Brown and nephew of Jim Brown, whom he so often tangled with at home. Dan had continued his family's outlaw legacy and was buying gold from the miners with counterfeit currency from the Missouri State Bank. According to legend, the estimated $200,000 taken from the miners was buried somewhere near the area where the Jim Brown Gang operated in Summit County. This stash would also have a current value in the millions. The last time any money was recovered was in 1865 when a can containing $4,000 was found by some school-aged children.

The last hidden treasure is said to be at the former location of the Bellevue War in Iowa. After the bloody shootout, it was rumored that bodies and property were thrown into a well on the property. Some of that property included gold and other valuables that were unknowingly discarded. The well was later filled up and the bodies never discarded. A syndicated newspaper article from 1898 reports that years after the war, an unidentified associate of the hotel owner wandered onto the property begging permission to dig up the old well. The man was believed to be the last survivor of the Bellevue War, but his identity was never revealed.

If there is truth to any of these rumors about buried money, it would be virtually impossible to find. Most of these swamps no longer exist, and there is no other traceable evidence where it can be found. Anyone with first-hand knowledge of where this fortune can be found has been buried almost as long as the money itself. With the help of this book, the loot will be buried much longer than the stories of how this band of organized thieves and counterfeiters helped settle the Midwest.

APPENDIX A
IDENTIFIED ORGANIZED CRIME ASSOCIATES

Aikens, Charles Fled Ogle County to Fort Madison, Iowa. Was assaulted after a confrontation with the local residents and died from his injuries after being tied to a log and thrown in the Mississippi River.

Aikens, Richard Died from exposure in the 1840's after spending extended hours outside hiding from Regulators.

Aikens, Samuel Father of Charles, Richard, and Thomas Aikens. Moved from Ogle County to Linn County, Iowa, and died in 1847.

Aikens, Thomas Rarely seen again after the execution of John Driskel Sr. Rumors that he settled up the Missouri River and spent the rest of his life as a farmer after escaping from jail.

Aker (?) Lived eight miles east of Coldwater, Michigan, and dealt in stolen horses.

Aldrich (?) Identified as Samuel Cluse, one of the largest counterfeiters in Missouri.

Alston, Peter Son of Philip Alston and responsible for the murder of blackleg Samuel Mason.

Alston, Philip Counterfeiter from South Carolina who moved throughout the United States and was likely the first head of the Blacklegs.

Ashley, William Went by the title of Colonel and was one of the original counterfeiters in Summit County, Ohio.

Atken, Thomas Broke out of jail in Monmouth, Illinois.

Avery, Philander Charged with larceny in Nauvoo, Illinois.

Avery, Samuel Charged with larceny in Nauvoo, Illinois.

Baker (?) Lived near Penn Yan, New York, and bought stolen property from Gregor McDougall and Sherman Mallet.

Barcus, Henry Associate of Napoleon Latta from Michigan who dealt in counterfeit.

Barlow, Jonathan Charged in Nauvoo, Illinois with horse stealing.

Belden, James Member of the Sturdivant Gang from Illinois.

Benton, Nelson Charged with larceny in Nauvoo, Illinois.

Bevington, Henry Indicted for stealing horses in Lagrange County in March 1858.

Birch, Robert One of the men involved in the Davenport Murder, he later fled to Arizona and New Mexico. He became a member of the Arizona Rangers and served under Second Lieutenant James Tevis to rid the Arizona Territory of outlaw gangs.

Blackman, Harrison (AKA Rollins) Involved in galvanizing counterfeit coin, associate of Simeon Webster.

Bliss, Adolphus Sentenced by the Lee Circuit Court in Iowa for robbery to a 3-5 year term, and died in prison.

Blowes, John Involved in the murder of John Nelles with William Townsend. Executed while he was still a teenager in front of the Cayuga Courthouse in Canada.

Bradley, Jefferson Charged with larceny in Nauvoo, Illinois.

Bridge, William K. Associate of John Driskel in Ogle County. He fled to Iowa and was killed by a sheriff.

Brock, Daniel Indicted for stealing harnesses in Lagrange County. The crime was witnessed by Miles Payne.

Brown, Issac A doctor from Kalamazoo, Michigan, who encouraged Samuel Cluse to engage in counterfeiting.

Britt, Jack Associate of the Driskels and resided in Stark County, Illinois.

Britt, William Associate of the Driskels and resided in Stark County, Illinois.

Brody, Hugh Operated in Ogle County, Illinois, but later fled to Linn County, Iowa.

Brody, John Sr. Originally from Franklin County, Ohio. Associate of John Driskel, fled to Linn County, Iowa, after the execution of John and William Driskel.

Brody, John Jr. Fled to Linn County, Iowa, after the execution of John and William Driskel.

Brody, Stephen Operated in Ogle County, Illinois but later fled to

Linn County, Iowa.

Brooks, Ben Ran a horse-thief ferry with his sons in Iowa.

Brown, (?) Participant in the murder of John Nelles. Turned state's evidence and spent the rest of his life in prison.

Brown, James 'Jim' Head of the James Brown Gang from Summit County, Ohio.

Brown, Thomas Involved in the murder of John Miller with the Hodges brothers.

Brown, William W. Owner of Brown's Hotel in Bellevue, Iowa, where the Bellevue War occurred. Killed during the shootout there with vigilantes.

Bryson, William Involved in the murder of John Nelles with William Townsend. Served the rest of his life in the Kingston Penitentiary.

Buell, Archie Resident of South Bend, Indiana, who worked as a blacksmith. Buell bought and sold counterfeit coin.

Burnham, Malcom Sentenced to 2 years in prison by US District Court in Indianapolis Counterfeiting. Previously escaped charges in Michigan and took all the counterfeiting dies with him and made his home in Noble County, Indiana. Other members of the gang went to serve time at the State Prison in Michigan.

Caldwell, William Member of the Sturdivant Gang from Illinois.

Campbell, Darius Accused of stealing a horse in Des Moines, Iowa. Also a brother-in-law to the Hodges.

Caruthers, John Identified counterfeiter who lived in Muscatine County, Iowa.

Cassiday, Walter Horse thief taken into custody with Ed Soper and Alonzo Gleason. Found in possession of a stolen horse at the time of his arrest.

Chamberlain, Dr. Associate of Blackleg John Wilson from the Fort Wayne area.

Champlin, Erastus Convicted in the Michigan Railroad Conspiracy case.

Champlin, Lyman Convicted in the Michigan Railroad Conspiracy case.

Champlin, Willard Convicted in the Michigan Railroad Conspiracy case.

Childs, Mark Charged with buying and receiving stolen goods in Nauvoo, Illinois.

Clark, James Baggage master in Fort Wayne who dealt in counterfeit.

Cluse, Samuel Known counterfeiter originally from Virginia. Broke out of jail in Michigan and traveled throughout Iowa and Missouri counterfeiting. Sentenced to five years in the Alton Penitentiary.

Clute, C.W. Fled from the same area as Alonzo Gleason.

Conklin, Peter Reportedly shot and killed by Regulators who were in pursuit of Alonzo Gleason.

Conlogue (?) Associate of Stephen Brody in Cedar County, Iowa.

Core / Gore, Hank Robbed a peddler with McDougall and other co- defendants, and hid the goods. Stole a guy named Storm's buggy, and stole guns with McDougall and Sol Stout.

Corwin, William Convicted in the Michigan Railroad Conspiracy case.

Cothrell, Jed Kept a saloon in the Fort Wayne area called 'Mad Anthony's Saloon.' He was known to deal in counterfeit money.

Crew, Joseph Noble County resident involved in buying counterfeit money.

Curtis, Asa Known counterfeiter from Missouri and an associate of Samuel Cluse.

Curtis, Perry Associate of Samuel Cluse who escaped from jail in Michigan after being arrested for counterfeiting.

Curtis, Truman Known counterfeiter from Missouri and an associate of Samuel Cluse.

Cutter, Joel Known to deal in counterfeit money and was a resident of Fort Wayne.

Dalton, William Indicted in 1851 for stealing horses in Lagrange County.

Davis, "Big" Broke out of jail in Monmouth, Illinois, and a known associate of the Driskels.

DeCourcey/Descoursey, Jonathan Suspected of being the individual who engraved the printing plates used to make counterfeit money.

Defore, Fred Resident of South Bend, Indiana, who worked as a Blacksmith. He was known to buy and sell counterfeit coin.

Deems, John Stole three horses with Shearer. Known to live in bothLagrange and Noble Counties.

Dewey, Corydon Sentenced from the Lee Circuit Court for robbery to a 3-5 year term.

Dewey, Daniel Miller Associate of Adolphus Bliss who was tried and sentenced to the Alton Penitentiary. Returned to his home and lived the remainder of his life as a farmer.

Donegan, D.I. Passed counterfeit money, and reportedly knew where to get counterfeit money in Ohio County, Indiana.

Doty, Silas One of the key figures in Blackleg history who operated throughout the United States and Mexico.

Drake (?) Part owner of a Drake & Woodwards Tavern east of Lagrange. He was known to deal in stolen goods, and bought stolen horses from Charles Smith.

Driskel, John Escaped from the Ohio Penitentiary, lived in Steuben County with the Sile Doty Gang before branching to Ogle County, Illinois, with his sons.

Driskel, David Son of John Driskel, murdered Regulator Chief John Campbell in Ogle Co with his brother Taylor.

Driskel, Pierce Convicted of murder by the Regulators but was released out of sympathy for his age. Previously served time in the Ohio Penitentiary for a crime that was actually committed by his father John Driskel Sr. Moved to Cook County, Illinois, after his father's execution and lived the remainder of his life there.

Driskel, Taylor Son of John Driskel, murdered Regulator Chief John Campbell in Ogle Co with his brother David.

Driskel, William Son of John Driskel, executed by Regulators with his father for murdering the head of the Regulators in Ogle County. Reportedly confessed to killing six men.

Duff, John Learned how to counterfeit from James Sturdivant and was one of the original settlers at Cave-in-Rock. Killed by Native Americans in 1804.

Eames, Nathaniel Charged in Nauvoo, Illinois with counterfeiting coins.

Farnham, Ebenezer Convicted in the Michigan Railroad Conspiracy case.

Field, Lewis Member of the Sturdivant Gang involved in passing counterfeit money.

Filley, Ammi Associate of Abel Fitch who was convicted in the Michigan Railroad Conspiracy case.

Finley (?) Resident of Adams County, Indiana, who lived between Decatur and Bluffton. He was known to store stolen horses.

Fleming, Alexander Former Adams County Sheriff, Blackleg, and was scheduled to be executed. He was charged with arson and forgery in Lagrange County, which was witnessed by Miles Payne.

Flinn, J. Involved with Simeon Webster manufacturing bogus coin.

Forsyth (?) Identified in Blacklegs' confessions as a person who sold stolen goods.

Fosket (?) Known counterfeiter from Rock Island, Illinois, who was reportedly talented with metals.

Fowler, John Known associate of Samuel Cluse and involved in counterfeiting in Iowa.

Fox, (?) (Aka Sutton) Either an associate of Robert Birch from Illinois or another alias name used by him.

Freeland, Andrew Convicted in the Michigan Railroad Conspiracy case.

French, Davis One of the first Blacklegs taken into custody by the Regulators.

Garmire, Jacob Bought counterfeit money from William Hill.

Garmire, William Bought counterfeit money from William Hill.

Gleason, Alonzo Horse thief and associate of Edward Soper, who was lynched by Regulators in Iowa.

Gay, George Washington Witness in the Michigan Railroad Conspiracy case who was an associate of Sile Doty.

Gilchrist, David Dealt in counterfeit money, indicted in Lagrange County in January 1858.

Goodrich, John Kept stolen horses and deals in counterfeit in Lagrange County.

Gowers, Sam Dealt in counterfeit money in Fort Wayne, kept stolen horses.

Green, Joseph Engraver who worked for the Sturdivant Gang in Illinois.

Green, Samuel Known associate of Samuel Cluse from Canton, Missouri, who was involved in counterfeiting.

Hadley / Headley (?) Robbed a peddler with McDougall and other co-defendants, and hid the stolen property.

Halberts, Sirus Member of the Sturdivant Gang from Cave-in-Rock, Illinois. A warrant for his arrest was issued for counterfeiting in 1823.

Hall, Joseph Blackleg identified in confessions.

Hammon, John Bought counterfeit money from Malcom Burnham.

Harpe, Micajah "Big" Part of the gang from Illinois and was the first serial killer in the United States along with his cousin Wiley Harpe.

Harpe, Wiley "Little" Part of the gang from Illinois and was the first serial killer in the United States along with his cousin Micajah Harpe.

Harrison, Charles E. Charged with counterfeiting in St. Joseph County, Michigan.

Hays, Ebenezer Member of the Sturdivant Gang from Cave-in-Rock, Illinois. A warrant for his arrest was issued for counterfeiting in 1823.

Helmer, Stephen Dealt in counterfeit in Lagrange County and was eventually indicted on those same charges.

Hibbard, Charles Tavern keeper, unknown location west of Indiana. Dealt in counterfeit money.

Hickman, William Charged with larceny in Nauvoo, Illinois.

Hiler, Charles Robbed a Morrow County man with John 'Flying Dutchman' Wilson.

Hill, Henry Present when the order was given by William Driskel to murder John Campbell. Testified in the trial held by the Regulators against John and William Driskel.

Hill, William D Harbored stolen goods from Red-Head and Charles Smith, counterfeited money. Hill went by the alias name of Townsend, reportedly organized the Blacklegs in Canada. He was also one of the Blacklegs' leaders in northeast Indiana. Last seen when he escaped from the Noble County Jail.

Hine, John Ran a horse-thief ferry with his father-in-law Ben Brooks.

Hodges, Amos Associate of Robert Birch who was involved in a robbery near Nauvoo, Illinois.

Hodges, Ervine Murdered by Return Jackson Redden for violating the code of silence.

Hodges, Stephen Involved in the murder of John Miller with his brother William, and was hanged for the crime in Iowa.

Hodges, William Involved in the murder of John Miller with his brother Stephen, and was hanged for the crime in Iowa.

Hogan, Samuel Lagrange County doctor, dealt in stolen goods.

Hoken, Ott Starch dealer, dealt in counterfeit. Possibly the same person as Ott Holcomb.

Holcomb, Ott Dealt in counterfeit money in Fort Wayne. Possibly the same person as Ott Hoken.

Holliday, Julius From Summit County, Ohio. Operator of the Old Stone House near Butler, Ohio, which was a haven for counterfeiters.

Holmes, Abraham Identified as an associate of Jim Brown in the Akron Buzzard, written by Sheriff Samuel Lane.

Holt, (?) Stole a horse in Lagrange County owned by a guy named Holsinger.

Howard, Edward Lived in Chemung County, New York, and bought stolen horses, robbed "Big Jim" with McDougall.

Huffman, Isaac Steuben County resident involved in buying stolen horses. Served time in the penitentiary. Gave John Wilson instructions on how to rob his father-in-law in Morrow County, Ohio.

Hunt, William Associate of John 'Flying Dutchman' Wilson from Defiance, Ohio.

Jackson, Sylvester Charged with counterfeiting coin in Nauvoo, Illinois.

Jackson, William Dealt in counterfeit money in Fort Wayne, and was one of the keepers of Mad Anthony's Saloon in Fort Wayne, Indiana.

Johnson, Artemus Involved in the murder of John Miller with the Hodges brothers.

Johnson, Lyman One of the original leaders of the Mormon Church (later excommunicated) who was an associate of Blacklegs in Illinois.

Johnson, Thomas Identified by Summit County Sheriff Samuel Lane as an associate of Jim Brown.

Johnson, William Associate of Robert Birch, murderer of Colonel George Davenport. They broke out of jail together in Knox County, Illinois.

Keeler, Joe Member of the Jim Brown Gang who lived in Portage, Ohio.

Kessler, Ed Robbed a Peddler with McDougall and other co-defendants, and hid the goods.

King, George Involved in the murder of John Nelles of Ontario. Caught and executed by Canadian authorities.

King, Joshua Member of the Jim Brown Gang who lived in Portage, Ohio.

Lane, Hank Accused of stealing horses in Nauvoo, Illinois.

Largehuft (?) Dealt in counterfeit money in Fort Wayne.

Latta, Napoleon Bonaparte Owner of a hotel east of Sturgis, Michigan. He abandoned the hotel in 1857 when brought up on counterfeit charges.

Latta, William ("Tamarack Latta") Mill Owner, dealt in counterfeit money, harbored stolen property and horses. He was identified as one of the leaders of the Blacklegs in northeastern Indiana.

Lattice, John Involved in the murder of John Nelles with William Townsend. He tried to escape Canada to the United States, but was shot and killed on the ice by a local constable. His name was also spelled Lettice.

Latty, Bone Son of William Latty. He was an associate of Sile Doty and was involved in the Michigan Railroad Conspiracy case.

Leach, James Member of the Sturdivant Gang from Cave-in-Rock, Illinois. A warrant for his arrest was issued for counterfeiting in 1823.

Lehr, Margaret Involved with Simeon Webster manufacturing bogus coin.

Leverich, Chancy Associate of the Brody's who built the first cabin in Vinton, Cedar County, Iowa.

Leverich, Joel "Bogus Coon" Associate of the Brody's who lived in Linn, Cedar County, Iowa, who bought property from the Brody family. He was also a resident of Lagrange County and indicted for assault and battery in 1832.

Literel, Sam Associate of the Brody's after they settled in LinnCounty, Iowa.

Long, Aaron Worked with John Driskel in Ogle County. Involved in the murder of Colonel George Davenport. He was caught and executed with his brother John and Granville Young.

Long, John Worked with John Driskel in Ogle County. Involved in the murder of Colonel George Davenport. He was caught and executed with his brother Aaron and Granville Young.

Lowther, Carmie Lived in Lagrange County, dealt in counterfeit and stolen horses. Once served as the local constable.

Mallet, Sherman Lived in Chemung County, New York. Broke into stores with McDougall.

Mansfield (?) Identified Samuel Cluse as one of the largest counterfeiters in Missouri.

Marvin, John Indicted for forgery and counterfeiting in Lagrange County in March 1858.

Mason, Samuel Part of the original gang in southern Illinois. He was killed by fellow Blacklegs and decapitated so they could collect a bounty.

Meaker (?) Involved in counterfeiting operations in northeastern Indiana.

McCoy (?) Harbored Blackleg fugitives, and stole goods in Lagrange County, Indiana, with Charles Smith.

McDougall, John Gregor's brother, was in Tamarack at least once. Believed to have fled to Iowa per a letter captured by the Regulators during their investigation.

McDougall, Lorne Brother to Gregor McDougall. Served time for stealing horses and attempted murder in Canada.

McDougall, Gregor "Blackhawk" Accused of two murders and was hung by the neck by Regulators in Ligonier, Indiana, in 1858

McDowell, William Associate of Charles Oliver Jr. from Rockford, Illinois. Arrested by Regulators in 1845.

Meeker, H.N. Involved in counterfeiting money in Lagrange County. Associate of Simeon Webster.

Metlock, Edward One of the original Blacklegs of Noble County.

Middleton, S.B. Noble County resident who sold counterfeit money.

Misner, Jeremiah Bought stolen goods from McDougall.

Mount, Aaron Convicted in the Michigan Railroad Conspiracy case.

Murrell, John Organized a band of thieves in Stark County, Illinois, and was an associate of the Driskels.

Musick, Samuel Charged with larceny in Nauvoo, Illinois.

Nevers, Edward Cincinnati resident who was a printer by trade. He gave information to CP Bradley on the whereabouts of Perry Randolph and George Ulmer.

Nimmons, Ad Signed counterfeit bills in Lagrange County.

Oliver, Charles Jr. Robbed a store in Delaware County, Ohio. Came very close to being elected Justice of the Peace in Rockford. Suspected of being a higher-ranking Blackleg in Winnebago County, Illinois.

Oliver, John Indicted for forgery in Lagrange County through the testimony of Miles Payne.

Owen, Robert Charged with larceny in Nauvoo, Illinois.

Owens, Jedidiah Charged with larceny in Nauvoo, Illinois.

Palmer, George Broke into Spencerville Store in Dekalb County with Miles Payne and John 'Flying Dutchman' Wilson.

Paternalistic, Bill Livery Stable owner in Fort Wayne known to deal in stolen horses.

Patterson, Garrett Identified as a Townsend Gang member in the Moore Letters which were written in the 1850's. Also identified in the record of the Townsend trial.

Payne, Miles C. Blackleg turned into a detective for the Regulators, broke into Spencerville Store in Dekalb County with George Palmer and John Wilson.

Pettit, Ethaw Charged in Nauvoo, Illinois with assault with intent to kill.

Phipps, Eli Shadrack Son of Jesse Phipps and connected with John and Aaron Long.

Phipps, Jesse Leader of Blacklegs in southwest Indiana and the father of twin brothers Eli and John Phipps.

Phipps, John Meshack Son of Jesse Phipps and connected with John and Aaron Long.

Phipps, William Brother of Jesse Phipps from North Carolina and assisted with Blackleg operations in southwest Indiana.

Pitts, James Lived in Pretty Prairie, Lagrange County, signed counterfeit bills.

Plumb, Jeremiah Charged with larceny in Nauvoo, Iowa, and was an associate of the Mormons of that city.

Price, Ebenezer Convicted in the Michigan Railroad Conspiracy case.

Price, Richard Convicted in the Michigan Railroad Conspiracy case.

Pullover, Samuel (Aka Pulver) Bought bogus money from William Hill in Huntertown, and passed and dealt counterfeit.

Randolph, Perry Leader of the Blacklegs in Noble County. Moved to Noble County from Bath, Medina County, Ohio, in 1832. Fled Noble County after initial Regulator arrests in 1858.

Redden, George Grant Native of Portage County, Ohio, who involved himself with the Iowa Blacklegs and was involved in Davenport murder.

Redden, Return Jackson Associate of Robert Birch and son of George Grant Redden. Murdered Ervine Hodges for breaking the code of silence.

Redden, William Harrison Involved in the Iowa Blacklegs and involved in Davenport murder.

"Red-head" Broke into a store with Charles Smith and was an associate of Gregor McDougall.

Rice, Ike One of the original Blacklegs of Noble County.

Richardson, E.C. Charged with buying and receiving stolen goods in Nauvoo, Illinois.

Roberts, Hiram Counterfeiter who turned himself in to Regulators in Linn County, Iowa, and was subsequently lynched.

Robertson, Jacob Member of the Sturdivant Gang who was arrested in 1822 on counterfeiting charges.

Robinson, Clayton Involved in robberies in St. Joseph County, Michigan. Turned state's evidence against Napoleon Latta.

Rollin, Joseph Dealt in counterfeit money in northeastern Indiana.

Rollins, D.H. Involved with Simeon Webster in manufacturing bogus coin.

Royce, Norton B. From Delaware Co, Ohio, and followed John Driskel to Ogle County, Illinois. Later arrested and broke out of jail in Missouri.

Romans, (?) Steuben County resident involved in buying stolen horses.

Rosenkraus, John From Bath, New York, dealt in counterfeit money.

Roy, William Robbed a Scotchman in New York with Mallet.

Sanford, Alvin Charged with larceny in Nauvoo, Illinois.

Sawyer, (?) Associate of Corydon Dewey from Illinois.

Scott, William Identified by Samuel Cluse as one of the largest counterfeiters in Missouri.

Sebra, Bob Known associate of Samuel Cluse from Canton, Missouri, who was involved in counterfeiting.

Shearer, Jim Noble County resident involved in counterfeiting money.

Sherman, John Arrested with Napoleon Latta in Monroe, Wisconsin, on counterfeiting charges.

Sherwood, William Known counterfeiter from Kalamazoo, Michigan.

Smith, Charles (Aka Jones) Stole Wright's Goods with a guy named Wilkinson.

Smith, Daniel Caught with stolen property in Nauvoo, Illinois.

Smitzer (?) Robbed a peddler with McDougall and other co-defendants, and hid the goods.

Smith, Erastus Convicted in the Michigan Railroad Conspiracy case.

Smith, Frank Brother of Theon Smith and was involved with counterfeiting in northeastern Indiana.

Smith, Theon Brother of Frank Smith and was involved with counterfeiting in northeastern Indiana.

Soper, Ed Associate of the Brody's from Cedar County, Iowa.

Spence, Andrew Counterfeiter who resided in Platte County, Missouri, and was an associate of Samuel Cluse.

Spence, John Counterfeiter who resided in Platte County, Missouri, and was an associate of Samuel Cluse.

Stearns (?) Involved in the robbery of William Mulford in Illinois.

Steele, "Captain" Member of the Sturdivant Gang who was arrested during a raid in 1822.

Stephens, Uriah Associate of Perry Curtis who dealt in counterfeit gold in Missouri.

Streeter, Thomas Associate of Napoleon Latta who lived in Wisconsin and dealt in counterfeit.

Stout, Soloman Associate of Gregor McDougall who was involved in robbery in northeastern Indiana.

Sturdivant, Azor Member of the Sturdivant Gang from Illinois and father of Merrick and Roswell Sturdivant.

Sturdivant, James "Bloody" Father of Azor Sturdivant and the original head of the Sturdivant Gang.

Sturdivant, Merrick Member of the Sturdivant Gang from Cave-in-Rock, Illinois. A warrant for his arrested was issued for counterfeiting in 1823.

Sturdivant, Roswell Member of the Sturdivant Gang from Illinois.

Sturdivant, Stephen Member of the Sturdivant Gang from Illinois.

Switzer, Henry Associate of the Brody's after they settled in Linn County, Iowa.

Sutton, Dr. Lagrange County doctor, killed himself with Laudanum after McDougall was hung.

Sutton (?) (Aka Fox) Associated with the blacklegs in Winnebago County, Illinois.

Taylor, Hawkins Lived in Nauvoo, Illinois and was a Blackleg sympathizer.

Taylor, Humphrey Uncle of John Taylor, who manufactured bogus coin in Peoria, Illinois.

Taylor, John A. Associate of Simeon Webster from Toledo, Ohio. Taylor had the recipes for making ordinary metal look like gold and silver. Associated with crooked judges and lawyers. Previously served time in the penitentiary.

Taylor, William G. Originally from Cleveland, worked as a lawyer, and identified as an associate of Jim Brown by Sheriff Samuel Lane.

Thomas, John Associate of Simeon Webster and John Taylor who manufactured bogus coin.

Thompson, Henry From New York, dealt in counterfeit money.

Thompson, John From New York, dealt in counterfeit money.

Thompson, Jonathan Lived in Kinsman, Ohio, and made bogus coins.

Thompson, William Former sheriff in Chemung County, New York, dealt in counterfeit money there.

Traxler, Daniel Brother-in-law to Gregor McDougall, involved in stealing horses near Wallaceburg, Ontario.

Turner, Elias From Ohio, reportedly hid out at Ulmer's after a jail break in the early 1840's.

Ulmer, George T One of the leaders of the Blacklegs of Noble County. Arrived in Noble County from Portage County, Ohio, in 1835. Also lived in Lagrange County.

Vanalstine, William Owner of a livery stable in Fort Wayne and known associate of Blacklegs there.

Vaughn, Charles Arrested with Napoleon Latta in Monroe, Wisconsin, on counterfeiting charges.

Vickers, Jonathan Charged with counterfeiting in St. Joseph County, Michigan.

Vrooman, David Ran a horse-thief ferry with Ben Brooks in Iowa.

Wait, Truman Involved in stealing a horse in Des Moines, Iowa, in 1842.

Walker, J. Noble County resident involved in counterfeiting coin.

Wallace, Lester Associate of the Brody's in Linn County, Iowa, arrested for robbery.

Weaver, (?) Identified as a Townsend Gang member in the Moore Letters, which were written in the 1850's. Died of tuberculosis.

Webster, Simeon Counterfeited money, lived in Noble County.

West, Charles Part of a branch identified as Dewey, West, and Bliss, which operated in Lee County, Illinois. Once appointed as constable.

Weston, Barney Broke into a store in Springfield with McDougall and Sol Stout.

Wheeler, Stephen Associate of Napoleon Latta who dealt in counterfeit.

Wickerson, Levi Charged with larceny in Nauvoo, Illinois.

Wilkinson (?) Stole Wright's Goods with Charles Smith, sold them to William Hill.

Williams (?) Identified by Samuel Cluse as one of the largest counterfeiters in Missouri.

Williams, Orlando Convicted in the Michigan Railroad Conspiracy case.

Wilson, Benjamin F Tavern keeper near Wrights Corners, Lagrange County. Dealt in counterfeit money in Lagrange County. Kept stolen horses for Miles Payne.

Wilson, Daniel Dealt in counterfeit money in Lagrange County.

Wilson, John "Flying Dutchman" Stole horses in Ohio and took them 35 miles north of Cincinnati. Broke into the Spencerville Store with Miles Payne and George Palmer. Lived in Lafayette, Ohio. After he fled Noble County, the Regulators offered a $400 reward for his arrest. Later arrested by US Marshal Elliot of Ohio. Later escaped from the Noble County Jail.

Woods, Jim Worked as an attorney for Blacklegs in Iowa.

Woodward (?) Part owner of a Drake & Woodwards Tavern four miles east of Lagrange, dealt in stolen goods. Also bought stolen horses from Charles Smith.

Young, Granville Worked with John Driskel in Ogle County. Involved in the murder of Colonel George Davenport. He was caught and executed with brothers John and Aaron Long.

Young, Sandy Known counterfeiter from Prairie Ronde, Kalamazoo County, Michigan.

Young, Thomas Blackleg who escaped from the custody of Regulators in Ligonier in March 1858. The Regulators offered a $300 reward for his capture.

APPENDIX B
REPORT FROM THE REGULATORS
INVESTIGATION ON GREGOR MCDOUGALL

The Regulators made the following report, which appeared in the History of the

Regulators, written by the Attorney M.H. Mott and published in 1900. It is a

summary of how the Regulators came to the decision of hanging McDougall for his

crimes:

The 26th of January, 1858, is a day long to be remembered by the citizens of Noble

and adjoining counties, as being the day on which was executed Gregory McDougall,

and we shall endeavor to give such facts as shall make the reader acquainted with all

the attending circumstances.

It is a well-known fact, that for years our County and Lagrange have been known,

hundreds of miles, as the dens of blacklegs of every conceivable grade; and honest

citizens, while from home, have hardly dared own their place of residence, for fear of

being looked upon as one not safe to run at large, and as the sequel will show, not

without cause. Years since, while our country was new and hiding places plenty, the

notorious Latte, Hill, Ulmer & Co., formed their nucleus near the Tamarack, as a

place to which all might meet to take counsel, lay plans, manufacture counterfeit money

and be safe from harm. For years their gang in a measure, controlled our election, sat upon our juries thus rendering the laws of no avail. Year after year has passed away and the same state of things has continued. Our horses, buggies, harness and other property, have been stolen by the wholesale; our stores broken and goods taken. Our citizens have been meet by the highwayman and at the pistol's muzzle robbed, and in one instance stabbed; and so well were their plans laid that their detection seemed impossible.

Thus, for years, have this bandits pursued their course. No man or his property was safe while this gang remained in our midst. If, by chance one was arrested, he would be released by his comrades, or break jail, go on inadequate straw bale, or if held to court, be sworn clear by his confederates under the alibi dodge, until our citizens lost all hopes as to the laws accomplishing the desired result.

By a chain of fortuitous circumstances, a short time since, the gang, their numbers and places of deposit, became known, when a Committee of Vigilance was formed to bring them to justice. The result was that some twenty-five were arrested, and of the number fourteen are now in jail, well-guarded. During the investigation it became known that one of the gang, a former accomplice of the notorious Townsend, one Gregory McDougall, alias Gregory McGregor, Geo. McLean, Geo. Bates, was in custody of the Court. A man who, by his own confession, was born in Wallaceburg, Kent County, Canada West, in the year 1831, where he commenced his career of crime by breaking the Chatham jail, where his brother was confined, robbing the jailors wife of a purse of gold; also robbing a schoolmaster of a watch on the ice, and names of other affairs in Canada, details which stamp him as one of the most desperate and hardened villains that the annals of crime present.

Since April last, he with two others, have stolen no less than thirty four horses, broke two jails, robbed four stores, and two tanneries, took the entire load of two peddlers, besides a large amount of harness, saddles, buggies, and other property too numerous to mention; who publicly boasted that no jail could hold him, and that he feared neither God, man or the devil. Further, there seems to be other and deeper acts, which he did not confess, and which we will briefly detail.

The Deputy U.S. Marshal of Michigan states, under oath, that he has had in his possession for some time, a reward form Canada for the apprehension of this man, for the crimes of robbing, an attempt to break jail and murder. McDougall confesses to his identity in the acts of robbing and attempt to break the jail at Chatham, Canada, to release his brother, but denies that the murder occurred. The Marshal, Mr. Halstead, however states that he went to Canada twice to investigate the matter, and that the murder was committed upon the very person that McDougall confesses of robbing, to-wit: the jailors wife of the prison , where McDowell's brother was confined. Added to this, we have the testimony of a confederate, taken separate and apart from the statement of the Marshal, that McDougall in relating his exploits, stated that those occurrences did take place, and that he gave the blow that caused death.

McDougall also confesses to robbing a schoolmaster on the ice but denies his murder. We have, from the same authorities and others, that the schoolmaster was not only robbed, but murdered and found dead on the ice.

One other crime we will mention, and close this harrowing and sickening detail. This former confederate, heretofore mentioned, states that McDougall informed him, that he and other accomplice, hearing of a Scotchman that had received quite a sum of money,

229

proceeded to rob him of the treasure. With pistol to their victim's breast they demanded
his money. He told them that he had deposited it in bank. After a search, and not
believing his statement, they proceeded to divest him of what clothing was necessary, and
procuring live coals roasted a fire upon them. They released him before death occurred,
becoming satisfied that their victim had told them the truth. McDougall, in his
confession, qualifies by saying, that he held his accomplices horses, while they did the
act. We leave our readers to judge of the executed man's complicity in these acts.

Proofs being positive, a jury of citizens, (not a jury of twelve, but a jury of hundreds,)
decided that justice required that he die; and on this memorable day he was executed;
not by a rabble, not by a nosy mob, not by young men in the heat of passion, but by
men who for years have been residents of this and the adjoining counties, - men that
were impelled, not by a thirst for blood, not to riot in the agonies of one made in the
image of the God they worshiped, but that stern justice be demanded the offering as an
example to the young in their midst, many of whom have already the solemnity of the
hour; all would have gladly have had it otherwise, if justice could have been satisfied
through any of other chancel; but all felt that his was the only resort. During the fore
part of the day he was visited by two clergymen, who endeavored to point his thoughts to
Him who holds the destinies of man in His keeping, and who is free to forgive all, even
to the most guilty.

Gregory McDougall was brought before the committee on the
evening of the 25th of January, when he was informed for the first time,
of the doom that awaited him – that he was to be executed the next day at
12 o'clock. The gentlemen whose duty it was to break him this painful

and unwelcome intelligence, addressed the prisoner in some very affecting and appropriate remarks, which seemed to affect him to such a degree that he appeared confused, and made some wandering remarks, such as "Well, gentlemen, I am in your power, deal with me as you see fit – I have never been in Canada – I never had a brother there". He said that he committed many thefts, and commenced to relate them, but was told that perhaps he had better return to his room, where if he had anything to relate – any confessions to make, he would be waited upon by two or three persons, who would commit to writing whatever he desired to communicate – to which he assented. He was then asked if he would like to have a clergymen visit his room and confer with him on spiritual matters. He replied that he would, and desired to know if he could not have an opportunity of seeing his wife. He was told that his wife should be sent for immediately. He was then taken back to his room, and the messengers dispatched at once for his wife and child, who arrive the next morning at 7 o'clock.

"After having made a full and fair investigation of all the testimony, and having found, during the said investigation, evidence of an unmistakable character, charging the said Gregory McDougall with murder, do recommend, that the said McDougall be hung the by neck until dead, on Tuesday, the 26the day of January, 1858, at 2 o'clock P.M. "

APPENDIX C
ORGANIZED REGULATOR COMPANIES OF
NORTHEASTERN INDIANA

Adams Township Rangers

Albion Rangers

Allen Reconnoiters

Angola Regulators

Bluffton Regulators

Cedar Creek Protectors

Cedar Lake Rangers

Concord Protective Band

Concord Rangers

Concord Regulator Association

Dekalb County Horse Thief Detecting Society

Dekalb County Vigilance Committee

Detective Association of Butler Township

Eden Police

Eel River Regulators

Fairfield Protectors

Fremont Rangers

Independent Self-Protectors

Jackson Prairie Horse Thief Detecting Society

Jackson Township Detective Association

Jackson Township Number One Order of Regulators Association

Jefferson Regulators

Kekionga Guards

Keyser Township Detective Association

Lafayette Rangers

Lagrange Association of Clearspring

Lagrange Self-Protecting Association

Lagrange County Rangers

Leesburg Horse Company

Ligonier Regulators

Lisbon Rangers

Marion Rangers

Mutual Protection Company

New Haven Vigilantes

Newville Rangers

Noble County Invincibles

Perry Regulators / Rangers

Plymouth Regulators

Police Guards

Port Mitchell Regulators

Perry Regulators

Protection Company of Newville

Richland Rangers

Saint Joseph County Mutual Protection Association

Saint Joe Detectives

Saint Joe Protective Association

Salem Horse Thief Detecting Company

Self-Protectors at Flint

Self-Protectors of South Milford

Self-Protectors of Springfield

Sparta Guards

Springfield Detectives

Springfield Spies

Stafford Mutual Protection Association

Swan Regulators

Union Detectives

Union Regulators

Warsaw Horse Thief Company

Wilmington Center Detectives

Wolf Lake Sharpers

APPENDIX D
ENACTMENT OF THE INDIANA GENERAL ASSEMBLY FROM MARCH 9, 1852

AN ACT entitled an act concerning the workings and institution of detective associations and repealing all laws and parts of laws in conflict therewith.

Horse Thief Detective Associations.

Section 1. *Be it enacted by the general assembly of the State of Indiana,* That any number of persons, citizens of the State of Indiana not less than ten and their associates and successors, to any number are hereby authorized to form themselves into companies for the purpose of detecting and apprehending horse thieves and other felons, and for mutual protection and indemnity against the acts of such horse thieves and felons, as hereafter provided.

Incorporation—Powers.

Section 2. That said association shall be incorporated under the voluntary corporation acts now in force in the State of Indiana and under the name and style designated in said articles during the continuance of this act, may sue and be sued, plead and be impleaded, answer and be answered, in any court of competent jurisdiction, and may have and use a common seal, and alter it at pleasure.

Officers of Association.

Section 3. Said corporation may appoint or elect all such officers as they may deem necessary for their organization, which shall severally hold their offices and perform the duties that may be required of them, either with or without compensation as their constitution and by-laws may direct.

Constitution and By-Laws.

Section 4. A majority of said corporation shall have power to adopt a constitution and by-laws for their government, and inflict such penalty as may be necessary to carry the same into effect, and enforce obedience to the same, which constitution and by-laws shall be consistent with the constitution and laws of this state and of the United States.

Section 5. Such number of persons of the said corporation as they shall designate in their constitution and by-laws shall form a quorum to transact all kinds of business, and sit upon their own adjournments or at the call of the president may at any time call such special meeting as may be necessary.

New Members—Expulsion.

Section 6. Said corporation may at any time add to their numbers in any way prescribed by their constitution and by-laws, and may expel members in such manner and for such cause as therein prescribed, and may receive donations in money or property, to be applied to the purposes of their organization, and may assess such dues, and impose such fines upon their members as shall be prescribed in their constitution and by-laws.

Aid of Peace Officers.

Section 7. Said corporation shall have power to call to their aid the peace officers of this state, in accordance with law, in the pursuit and apprehension of all felons and in reclaiming stolen property and restoring it to the owner or owners thereof.

Presiding and Other Officers—Power as Constable.

Section 8. A majority of the members of such association shall have power to adopt a constitution and by-laws for their government, to designate and appoint a presiding officer and such other officers as they may deem proper, who shall hold their offices for such time, and shall perform the duties required of them by such constitution and by-laws, and such presiding officer is hereby authorized and empowered to administer oaths to members of such association in all matters wherein oaths are necessary to be administered by the rules and by-laws of the association, and such association, with the consent of the board of commissioners of the county wherein the certificate of association is recorded, may designate any or all members of the association who during their term of appointment shall have all the power of constables, and such association shall furnish the board of commissioners a list of the names of members so designated, and if consent is given, the board shall enter upon its record an order reciting the names of such persons, and that the consent of the board has been given to such appointments, and the record so made shall authorize and empower the county auditor to issue to each member so designated a certificate of his appointment as constable: *Provided,* That such constables shall have power to pursue and arrest horse thieves and all other criminals against the laws of the State of Indiana, and to serve all papers relating to the same, and to follow and pursue such criminals in and through any part of the State of Indiana; and in the absence of warrant shall have power to arrest and hold in custody without warrant and for such time as may be necessary to procure a warrant.

Acts Legalized.

Section 9. All steps taken and acts done by any horse thief detective association or company organized under sections 4491 to 4495 inclusive, Burns' Revised Statutes of 1901, be and the same are hereby declared to be legal and valid: *Provided,* Nothing in this act shall affect any pending litigation.l.

Section 10. That all laws or parts of laws in conflict herewith are hereby repealed.

APPENDIX E
CONSTITUTION FOR THE IOWA PROTECTION SOCIETY (REGULATORS)

This Society shall be called the Iowa Protection Company.

Article 1. The object of this Society shall be to protect the property of the members of this company, and particularly their horses, from the depredations of robbers and thieves, and also to trace out the perpetrators of thefts, rescue and restore property stolen, and assist in a due and faithful administration of law and justice.

Article 2. The others of this Society shall consist of a President, Secretary and Treasurer, to be chosen, at stated meeting, and to hold their offices during good behavior.

Article 3. It shall be the duty of the President to preside at all regular meetings of the Society, and, in his absence, the Society may choose a President pro tem.; and it shall be the duty of the Secretary to record all the proceedings of the Society, and preserve the same ; and it shall

be the duty of each member to pay to the Treasurer such sums of money from time to time as the Society shall dictate. He shall keep a correct book in which he shall enter the amount received and expended, and the purpose for which it was expended.

Article 4. The Society shall appoint such committees as may be necessary to carry out the objects of the Society.

Article 5. Each and every member shall sign the constitution and hold themselves subject to its provisions, and on revealing its proceedings in any respect, shall be excluded from its benefits.

Article 6. This Society shall be convened at any time by notice from the President.

Article 7. No person shall be entitled to vote unless a member of the Society.

Article 8. This constitution may be altered or amended at any regular meeting, by a two-thirds vote of the members present.

Article 9. No person shall be admitted a member of this Society who is under suspicion of horse stealing or any other theft, or for harboring thieves or robbers.

Article 10. The regular meeting of this Society shall be the Saturday before the full of the moon, at such place as may be designated

APPENDIX F
CONFESSION OF BLACKLEG SAMUEL B. CLUSE,

Printed in the Illinois free trader, Ottawa, Illinois on April 28, 1842:

I, Samuel B. Cluse, having been lately convicted of a jury of my countrymen, of the crime of counterfeiting, and sentenced to be confined in the penitentiary for the period of four years, wish to make the following confession to the world, and in doing so, I have been actuated by two considerations: First, I wish to relieve my mind of the load of guilt that has long been treasured up within it, so far as I can do by a disclosure of my own crimes, and an exposure of those engaged in like criminal transactions – but I am now particularly influenced by a hope that, pursuing the course I am about to, I may be the means of turning others from their wicked ways, and by pointing out the rock upon which I have split, I may prove a warning to those who are now, as I once was, free from guilt.

I have no right to complain at my hard fate. I have been quite successful in the business I have followed as I had any right to expect; but, notwithstanding all my vigilance (which has been untiring) to evade justice, I have at length fallen into her jaws.

To give a detailed account of all my villainies, and to expose all who have been engaged with me from the commencement, is more than I have time now to do, and more than anyone would have patience to hear. I can now give but a brief sketch of my infamous career.

I was born in Loudon County, Virginia in the year of 1810. My father was a Quaker, and was formerly in good circumstances, but lost his property by going security for a friend. After this reverse of fortune, he moved to Michigan. I lived with him till I was 14 years of age. From fourteen to twenty-one I was raised by a tobacco merchant in Rushville, Ohio.

When I was eighteen years of age I got married to a young girl in Muskingum County, Ohio. This was the most unfortunate event in my life. I can only recur to it with pain at this distant period of time; and, had it no exercised such an important influence on my subsequent life, I would have passed it by unnoticed. I lived with my wife but two years, which two years consisted of anything but that domestic bliss that I had fondly imagined. At last her amours became both shameful and insupportable, and I abandoned her. During my sojourn with her conduct was such, that the only consolation I could find was in the intoxicating cup. I then contracted a habit which has clung to me ever since.

Soon after parting with my wife, I returned to my father's, where I lived for some length of time. From my parents I received much honest instruction. If my after life has been wayward, the guilt is on my own head, not theirs. Upon leaving my father, I embarked my traffic with Indians. About the same time, I engaged in counterfeiting. I was persuaded to engage in the business by Dr. Isaac Brown, William Sherwood, and Sandy Young of Prairie Round, Kalamazoo County, Michigan. They exhibited large quantities of spurious money to me, and told me of fortunes that had been made in the business. They discovered that I was disposed

244

to listen to their proposition, and appointed a place of meeting to consult further upon the subject. We met at Dick's Tavern on Big Prairie Round, there they renewed their argument to me to induce me to join them, with complete success. I went into the business and continued it for five years without being suspected. I was then taken up and imprisoned for making bogus. The way I was detected was this: A couple of fellows by the name of Acres and Harrington, living at Lafayette, Indiana stole a Baptist preacher's horse in partnership. Harrington brought the horse to Monticello, Michigan and there met Acres and made a sham sale to him in the presence of Perry Curtis and myself. Acres gave his note for the horse and I and Curtis witnessed it.

I then gave Acres of $5 bill on a Catskill Bank, New York, and four or five pieces of bogus and started him to sell the horse, though I was not in the original stealing. Acres passed the bill that I gave him at James Smith's store at Prairie Round, and then started for Kalamazoo. Smith, finding the bill spurious, pursued and caught him and carried him back. They then accused him of stealing the horse, and told him if he would expose the club with whom he was connected he should go clear. He did so, me among the others. An express was then sent to St. Joseph County to have us arrested. Perry Curtis, a man of the name of Osborne were in the house at the time. Curtis had gone out to bury the dies. They caught him with the shovel in his shoulder, but did not find the dies. They found, however, our plaster of Paris, and black steel dies, but no counterfeit money. We were then taken before a magistrate, and Acres was brought up as a witness against us. We were bound over and for want of bail, committed. After lying in jail three months a good friend from without passed me an augur with which I bored through what

245

we called the ten of diamonds, and with the shank of the augur picked the locks. Curtis escaped with me. I then went to Prairie Round and made a raise of $2,000 counterfeit money on the State Bank of Indiana and $500 in bogus, which I got of Captain Harrison and Lawyer Belcher.

The counterfeit paper was made at Albany, NY and was sent to Ypsilanti to Samuel Woodruff, filled up the bills. Woodruff had once been respectable and in good circumstances, was formerly teller of the bank, but became dissipated and took to counterfeiting. The bogus was made at Mottville, Michigan. After making this raise, I sloped for Iowa, and after leaving Prairie Round, I traveled in the night and kept concealed in the daytime. I was not seen by any person until I got to Edward Ruggles who lives six miles south of Chicago. I exchanged with him $300 of the money I had, and got the bills of the Albany Merchants and Mechanics Bank (there never was such a bank). I then went to Mr. King's, eighteen miles west of Chicago on the Dixon road. There I found an old friend of mine, we engaged the night in a big spree. They had heard of my being taken up and were both surprised and rejoiced at seeing me. I made lots of friends here, found the place deposit in the neighborhood at a man by the name of Aldrich. From there I came on to Dixon, and there met with a man who had contract on the railroad. I let him have $500 of my money. Upon leaving Dixon I came on down Rock River to Austin Williams, remaining with him three or four days. This was about the 1st of August 1839. I let Williams have $300 in bogus silver for which he was to give to me $35 per $100. He was called our western partner. While I was in his house, I heard that one of my friends was confined in Stephenson. I sold my horse of Williams, as I thought best to take it on foot. I then started for Stephenson to see my friend.

When I arrived there, I went to see my friend, whose name was Gregg. He and another fellow whose name was Shaver, were in irons. He asked me if I couldn't aid him in liberating himself. I told him I was not then in a situation to help him, but I thought I could send him a man that would. Greg told me that our old "bogus coon" Leveredge lived at Moscow, Iowa. I left Stephenson and went up to Fulton City where I crossed the Mississippi River, and sent Roswell Winn, one of his gang, to help out Gregg. Winn came down to Stephenson and furnished Gregg and Shaver with tools, with which they escaped. I made but a short stay with Bigelow but left for Moscow, as I was anxious to see the old bogus coon. On arriving at Moscow, I found he had moved to Linn County.

In conversation with people at Moscow, I found that the Stoughtonburgh members of our clan lived in Cedar County. I left Moscow and went on to Rochester, and there by signs I found out that the grocery keeper was a man of the right stripe for our business. I made some exchanges with him and he cautioned me to be very careful in inquiring for the Stoughtonburgh's. I found their character so notorious that I did not think it prudent to stay long with them, but went on to Westport, in Linn County. There I found Leveredge, the old bogus coon. He was very glad to see me, invited me into the grocery, and spent a bogus half dollar, as he said, for my sake. He made very good bogus, and has been long suspected, but they never could head him. On leaving Leveredge, I went to Mr. King whom I know in Michigan. King was an honest man, he knew what business I was engaged in, and advised me to quit it. He told me that he feared if I pursued in my course I should come to some bad end. I did not heed his advice, but hastened him and his moral lectures. Went to Leveredge and disposed of what money I had left. When I left there I had $400 in good money. At Marion, in Linn County, I fell in with a man by the name of Howard, who was a Campbellite preacher and counterfeiter. We left together for John Caruther's in Muscatine County. There I got $700 in ten dollar bills on the Merchants and Mechanics bank at Albany. From here we started to go to Portland, on the Des Moines and went within three miles of Mt. Pleasant. There we stopped for three days. Howard passed for a Baptist preacher and I for a Methodist. The people where we stopped were pious, and were anxious to have divine service while we stopped with them. We appointed an evening for preaching. . Howard preached and I closed the meeting with a prayer. Our hearers were so well pleased with the service that they prevailed on Howard to stop with them and take a school but I pushed onto Portland.

At Portland I entered upon my list of friends of justice of the peace whose name was Ferris and let him have $100 of my money. After remaining in Portland a few days, I left in company with John Fowler for Rock House Prairie, Platte Purchase, Missouri, where we arrived in September 1839. I had not been long here when I heard that my partner, Perry Curtis, who in will be recollected, broke jail with me in Michigan, was at work in a bogus factory about twelve miles distant. I lost no time in calling on him, found him in fine spirits. He said he was full of money and had met with great success since we parted at the jail in Michigan. I spent about a year in Missouri, part of the time in Platte Purchase, part up the Osage River, and part in Morgan County. As a minute account of all my doings while in that country would probably be useless as well as tedious, I must content myself with giving that part only which I think may be useful.

The Platte Country is one of the strongest hold of counterfeiters, horse thieves, and vagabonds of every die. It is the great focus where those who run from their country for their crimes congregate with impunity. It was very rare for one of our men to get "jerked up" in that country but what we got him clear, if false searing could do it, but that was not always necessary, for we had more than one stout friend a month the magistrates.

The most extensive operations in making bogus is carried on in the Platte Purchase hat I know of anywhere. I was engaged in coning in two large mints while I was there. Smith's mint which is the most extensive, is situated in the timber at the narrows, on the big Platte River, on the Platte side, twelve miles north of Oshaw's Mill, and one mile from the river. The coin which they make is mostly Mexican. The other establishment at which I work belonged to John and Andrew Spence, and is from one and a half to two miles west of Jamestown. The works are carried on in the cellar of the old stone house. I have been thus particular in pointing out their locality, that they may be hunted out and broken up. I could give a long account of the monkey shines I cut up while in the Platte country, but as it would be father amusing than of any utility, let that pass.

I left the Platte country in September 1840 and came to St. Louis. On my way I fell in company and traveled with an Irishman. He was a keen fellow, too keen for me. When we got to St. Louis I gave him a fifty dollar counterfeit bill on a New Orleans Bank to go and get changed but that was the last of him. I did not stay long at St. Louis but while I did stay I went it deep in the way of gambling, drinking, and other gentlemanly sports. Finding I was not making much in the line of my profession, I left for Canton, Fulton County, Illinois where I expected to meet my old friend Curtis. On my arrival at Canton I found that all the Curtis's had moved to Mercer. Before I got there Perry Curtis and his brother Truman had left for Platte Purchase, Missouri. Asa was my only home so I stayed with him but a few days to take breath and then took back track.

I went down to Des Moines River to Iowaville and there I tended grocery a while. But that I did not much like for though I could get as much good liquor as I could drink, yet I felt as if I was cramping my genius too much. I preferred patrolling the country and playing off my tricks upon the good and unsuspecting people whose fortune it was to fall in my way, so I left the grocery and came down to Farmington to see Dr. Lee who was an old hand at the bellows. The doctor told me that his stock of counterfeit had exhausted, but that he was expecting a large consignment in a few days with which he would supply me if I would stop until it arrived; but as I was anxious to see my friend Curtis, who, I understood, had returned to the Pope River. I did not wait its arrival but came up on to Curtis'.

On my arrival at Asa Curtis house I found Truman Curtis and Powell Holmes there. They had with them $150 in spurious gold. There were four of us in all, Truman Curtis, Powell Curtis, a fellow by the name of Cogswell, and myself. We lurked about Quincy for some days passing our gold when we could, and making such trades as were advantageous. We came near being detected once or twice while we were here by blunders of Cogswell. We found him such a fool that it was dangerous to have him with us, so we slipped off slyly to St. Louis and left him at Quincy. At St. Louis we got acquainted with a fellow who passed as Dr. Smith, and who boarded at the Virginia Hotel. Smith let us have $500 to dispose of on commission; he advised us to take a trip to Prairie Du Chien, and we did so but we found it a rather bad operation, for money was so badly executed that we were notable to pass some of the gold I had left. I passed only about enough to pay my expenses. I had not long been at Mercer when I received a letter from Perry Curtis, who was then in Missouri, he wanted me to go to Canton and see what I could do towards making sale of the gold which he was going to fetch on. I lost no time, put off immediately for Canton and as soon as I got there, I called on our friend Salmon Green and Bob Sebra. We held a counsel and determined who we should take into our crowd. After I got matters pretty well arranged Curtis arrived with the gold. We then commenced to disposing of it, we let Bob Sebra have $500 in gold and $50 bill on the Cape Fear Bank. He was to give us fifty dollars a hundred for the gold, and fifteen for the bill, and was to pay us the next day but never has paid.

Bob Sebra is suspected of being engaged in counterfeiting, but they never could defeat him. If a search could be made of his house, not forgetting his wife's petticoats, he would be very apt to be caught upon a hook that he could not get away from. We also disposed of some of our gold to some young men at Canton, but I forbear to give their names. I did it for a reason. I believe this to be the first impropriety of the kind of which they have been guilty, and I trust to see how badly I have fared they will take warning without having their names held up to the public gaze. I am also inducted to withhold their names from the great respectability of their parents, whose feelings I should be sorry to lacerate unnecessarily. My doings at Canton, it will be recollected by those who were

251

present at my trial, were alluded to by Mr. Kellogg. He was right when he said that "the experienced counterfeiter knew full well who to offer his money to, and to whom to throw out his lure. It is not for the man of experience of our business, but it is for the youth who knows little of the world or its dangers that he sets his trap."

Before I left Canton, Perry Curtis wanted me to take some of the gold to Allwood and sell to him, but I declined as I regarded it unsafe to have anything to do with so great a numbskull as I knew him to be. Curtis however, did not think as I did, but made a trade with him, he had occasion to rue it, afterwards Allwood turned State's evidence.

Leaving Perry Curtis at Canton, Truman and myself returned to Mercer County. Truman and Uriah Stephens then took a team and went back to Canton, and got some liquor and other things which he had bought there, and brought them on to Mercer. When they got back, Truman and myself took a trip to Blackhawk, Iowa to see Dr. Austain and William Searls. We took $100 in gold with us. With $250 of it we bought a horse. Curtis took the horse and returned to Mercer and I went out to pay my old friend, and friend of counterfeiters generally, John Caruthers a visit. On my return to Mercer I heard that Perry Curtis and Stephens had been arrested at Canton. $600 of the gold now remained. I and Mansfield started for Austin Williams to dispose of it. This was Mansfield's debut. He had known that I was in business for months, but this was the first venture and I reckon he will find so little sport in it, that it will be his last. But as I was saying we went to Williams. Austin was not at home but his brother was. We set upon the fence and had a long talk together. I wanted him to take the gold I had and give me a receipt for it, but he said he was afraid to do it. For that now-a-days he hardly knew his friends. He spoke of the Comanche robbery, and said they had been suspected of having stolen goods in their possession and he knew not what moment the officers of justice would be upon them to search their premises, and if said he, we should be found with this gold upon us, it would be rather of billions case for us and we might not easily get away from it. Taking all the circumstances into consideration, we concluded we would not leave the money but come off down the river taking it with us. We stopped at Brandenburgh's under the pretense of getting a drink. We felt at first we were suspected but from the way Brandenburgh talked with us, we afterwards came to the conclusion that our fears were groundless. So we came coolly down the river to Mr. Beals who lives on Mr. Cause's farm. I do not think Mr. Beals suspected us for counterfeiters. We stayed with him over night, and here we were overtaken the next morning by Mr. Atkinson and his company of "Regulators", who took us into custody and brought us to Rock Island. I have been tried, found guilty, and sentenced to the penitentiary for four years, an having given up all hopes of escape, I expect in a few days to be safely in Alton.

There are a great many connected in the business of counterfeiting, with whom I am acquainted, whose names are not mentioned in this confession. I called the other day, the names I knew to be thus engaged, and Mansfield keeping count. We made out over three hundred, Aldrich's, Williams', Caruther's, and William Scott's on the Des Moines are amongst the most noted harbors for counterfeiting.

Williams is known from the Platte country to Detroit. Of those near here who are more or less engaged in counterfeiting, may be reckoned. Messers, Fosket and Stephens, late of Rock Island, Cunningham of Hendersonville, Nelson Sischo and Van Burkin of Mercer County. Fosket is a scientific counterfeiter I was here at Rock Island in the summer saw and had a long talk with him. He worked upon the engine of the old Brazil. He then told me he had found out a new composition with which he could make the very best of bogus, and that he should go at it largely in a few days. Said he had all the implements for bogus making at Mr. Hales above Penna. Fosket is a man of great ingenuity and talents to fit him for any business. He was formerly a licensed Methodist preacher in Ohio but for some villainy, he was taken up and confined in jail a lower Sandusky, broke out and came west. At the time I saw him in the summer, he made his brags that he had his license to preach in his pocket. I have been thus particular in speaking of him, because, I think him one of the most dangerous men. He always has a large stock his possession and can make a key to order at any time and if any friend of his gets into a scrape, he can generally devise some means to get him out of it. I understand that he had left town at the time I was arrested, otherwise I should have had some assistance from him.

Uriah Stephens was in company with Perry Curtis, when he brought on the gold from Missouri. He was taken up as before remarked with Curtis, at Canton, but got clear for some cause or other. He and his family have been living here in town since I have been confined I prison, but learn that he left and is now living near Davenport, Iowa.

Cunningham is largely engaged in the business. He told me he had a large quantity of the bills of the Penn Bank of Pennsylvania, not yet signed, and that he also had the plates.

I have gone through with pretty much all I have to say. Such a mass of dry detail, I am aware cannot be very interesting, but I hope it may be of some utility. The crime of counterfeiting is becoming quite too common in the west, as many a young man raised to honorable notions of propriety, has been like me drawn into the vortex of the old and hardened counterfeiter, and ruined forever. It is those who are in the way of temptation, who have as yet a clear conscience that I wish particularly to address myself. Beware O! young man how you listen to the representation of the counterfeiter. He may tell you that his is the primrose path but let me tell you that path is lined with thorns. If you once permit yourself to listen to those representations, you will find to your sorrow, that the descent to the lowest sink of degradation is very easy. For years past I have hardly enjoyed a moment's conscious security, nor have I scarcely during that period laid down to rest, but what I have thought of being awakened by some officer.

Since I have been in jail I have uniformly received kind treatment. Today when I was seized with vertigo and almost frantic with pain, I had only to make known the feat when I was furnished with an extra pillow which to rest my fevered head.

The time is at hand for my departure to Alton, and I will only add a repetition of what I have before expressed, I hope my example may not be entirely lost upon the world.

SOURCES

(Please note that very few articles from early newspapers included the writer's name. In addition, many of the newspaper dates or pages were not legible due to the deterioration and issues with the original copies)

A Counterfeiter Hung (1858, January 29) *Indianapolis Daily Journal*, p.2.

A Distinguished Counterfeiter (1846, September 25) *Alton Telegraph and Democratic Review*, p. 1.

A Gang of Banditti (1858, January 20) *Goshen Democrat*, p.2.

A Great Criminal! (1841, April 20) *Mohawk Courier*, p.1.

A Short Sentence (1861) *The Journal of Lowville New York*, p.1.

Allen, J. (2010) *It Happened in Southern Illinois.* Southern Illinois University Press.

An Exposition. The Pardon of Perry Randolph: Who is Responsible? (1860, February 24) *Dawson's Daily Times*, p. 2.

An Unexampled Career of Crime (1857, December 9) *Sacramento Daily Union*, p.1.

Ander, O.F. (1959) Law and Lawlessness in Rock Island Prior to 1850, Journal of the Illinois State Historical Society, Winter (Vol. 52 No. 4).

Another Horse Thief Hanged (1857, December 25) *Janesville Daily Morning Gazette*, p.1.

Arrest of the Notorious Townsend, the Canadian Murderer and Highway Robber (1857, April 22) *Wayne Democratic Press*, p.2.

Astounding Disclosures – Robbery and Murder (1845, August 3) New York Herald, p.1.

Aurner, C. (1910) *Topical History of Cedar County, Iowa*. Chicago: The S.J. Clarke Publishing Company.

Black, P. (1912) *Iowa Journal of History and Politics, Volume X.* Iowa City, Iowa: The State Historical Society of Iowa.

Blacklegs are Congregated (1862, February 4) *Dawson's Daily Times and Union*, p.1.

Bonney, E. (1845) *The Murderers of Colonel Davenport.* National Police Gazette, p.114.

Brown, the Akron Counterfeiter (1846, August 18) *Huron Reflector*, p.2.

Butts, E. (2006) *The Desperate Ones: Forgotten Canadian Outlaws.* Toronto, Canada: Dundurn Press.

Clark, D. (1917) *Samuel Jordan Kirkwood.* Iowa City, Iowa: The State Historical Society of Iowa.

Common Pleas Verdict (1861, March) *Dawson's Fort Wayne Weekly News*, p.1.

Confessions and Crimes of a Canadian Youth (1858, June 18) *The New Era* (Canada), p.1.

Continued Excitement in Noble, A Man Actually Hung! (1858, January 27) *Goshen Democrat*, p.2.

Convictions for Murder at Cayuga, Canada (1855, May 3) *The Buffalo Courier*, p.1.

Correspondence of the Evening Post (1841, July 15) *New York Evening Post*, p.2.

Correspondence of the Evening Post (1841, July 31) *New York Evening Post*, p.2.

Counterfeiter Arrested (1868, December 8) *Syracuse Daily Journal*, p.1.

Douglass, Ben (1878) *History of Wayne County, Ohio from the Days of the Pioneers and First Settlers to the Present Time.* Indianapolis, Indiana: Robert Douglass, Publisher.

Drapier, A. & Drapier, W. (1859) *Legislative Reports: Embracing short-hand sketches of the Journals and Debates of the General Assembly of the State of Indiana.* Indianapolis: Daily Indiana State Sentinel.

Eliminating Lawlessness in Ligonier – McDougall Execution (1916, January 30) *Fort Wayne Journal Gazette,* p.1.

Goodspeed, W. (1882) *Counties of Whitley and Noble, Indiana.* Chicago: F.A. Battey & Co., Publishers.

Execution of the Murderers of Colonel Davenport at Rock Island, Illinois – Confession – Horrible Catastrophe (1845, November 27) *Ononadaga Daily Standard,* p.1.

False Seniments (1851) The Middlebury Register: Middlebury Vermont, Volume XVI, October 22, 1851.

Finley, A. (1851) *The History of Russellville and Logan County, Kentucky.* O.C. Rhea Publishing.

Gang of Counterfeiters Arrested! (1851, April 23) *Sandusky Clarion*, p.1.

George Randolph (1859, October 19) *Dawson's Fort Wayne Weekly Times*, p.1.

Great Excitement in Noble County! 1000 Horsemen in the Town of Ligonier! Arrest of Horse Thieves, Counterfeiters, and Murders. Man Hung Without the Benefit of Judge or Jury (1858, February 2) *Indianapolis Daily Journal*, p.2 .

Great Excitement in Noble County (1858, January 23) *Fort Wayne Sentinel*, p.1.

Greene, M. (1957) *The 'Self-Made' Outlaw of Toledo War Era*. Toledo: Toledo Blade, Published August 4, 1957.

Griswold, B. (1917) *Pictorial History of Fort Wayne, Indiana*. Chicago: Robert O. Law Company.

Guthrie, J. (1965, October 13) *Laws and Vigilantes*. Greensburg Daily News, p. 6.

Hall, J. (1916) *Stark County Illinois and its People.* Chicago: The Pioneer Publishing Company.

Highest Point Between Atlantic and Mississippi Located in Noble County (1916, January 30) *The Fort Wayne Journal-Gazette*, p.3.

Hirschfeld, C. (1953) *The Great Railroad Conspiracy, The Social History of a Railroad War.* Chicago, Illinois: R.R. Donnelley & Sons Company.

History of Benton County, Iowa (1878) Chicago: Western Historical Company.

History of Butler County, Pennsylvania (1883) Chicago: Waterman, Watkins & Co.

History of St. Joseph County, Michigan (1877) Philadelphia: L.H. Everts & Company.

History of Winnebago County, Illinois (1877) Chicago: H.F. Kett & Company.

263

Hopkins, J. (1959) *The Papers of Henry Clay, Volume 1*. Lexington: University of Kentucky Press.

Howe, H. (1888) *Historical Collections of Ohio, Volume II*. Cincinnati, Ohio: C.J. Krehbiel & Co., Printers and Binders.

Indiana Regulators (1858, February 8) *Allen County Democrat*, p.1.

Indiana Regulators (1858, June 21) *New York Times*, p.2.

Indiana Secretary of State Petitions (1838) Indiana Secretary of State, Indiana Digital Archives.

Kaler, S. & Maring, R. (1907) *History of Whitley County, Indiana*. Indianapolis: B.F. Bowen & Co., Publishers.

Kett, H. (1878) *The History of Ogle County, Illinois*. Chicago: H.F. Kett & Company Publishers.

Kildare, M. (1971) *Silas Doty Outlaw Loot*. Treasure Magazine, Vol. 2, Number 4. Canoga Park, CA: Modern Cycle Publishing.

Lane, S. (1892) *Fifty Years and over of Akron and Summit County*. Akron, Ohio: Beacon Job Department.

Leland, T. (1851) *Argument of William H. Seward in Defense of Abel F. Fitch and Others under an Indictment for Arson*. Auburn, NY: Derby and Miller.

Lynch Law in Full Force (1841, July 20) *Reflector News*, p.1.

Mail Robber (1841, December 23) *The Buffalo Courier*, P.2.

Mail Robber (1841, December 24) *New York Evening Post*, p.2.

McNally, B. (1879) *The History of Jackson County, Iowa*. Chicago, Illinois: Western Historical Company.

Mitchell, W. (1860, October 6) Dawson's Fort Wayne Daily Times, Letter to the Editor p.1.

Monks, L. (1916) *Courts and Lawyers of Indiana.* Indianapolis, Indiana: Federal Publishing Co., Inc.

Moore Letters (c. 1850) Norwich and District Archives, Norwich & District Historical Society, accessed from http://www.norwichdhs.ca/Moore%20letters%201850s Accessed May 1, 2013.

More Hanging of Horse-Thieves (1857, July 8) Davenport Gazette, p.1.

More Lynch Law in Iowa. The Excitement Increases, Three Men Killed (1857, July 7) *New York Herald*, p.1.

Mott, M. (1859) *History of the Regulators.* Indianapolis, Indiana: Indianapolis Journal Company.

Nelson, R. (1998) *The Raid on Sturdivant's Fort*. Springhouse Magazine, April 1998. Herod, Illinois.

Obituary of Christian Heltzel (1902, February 15) *Fort Wayne Sentinel*, p.1.

Pickett, A. (1851) *History of Alabama, and Incidentally of Georgia and Mississippi, from the Earliest Period*. Sheffield, Alabama: R.C. Randolph Publishing.

Re-Arrest of Royce the Counterfeiter (1845) *National Police Gazette*, p.254.

Republican Compiler (1823) June 18, 1823, Page 2, Gettysburg, Pennsylvania.

Riddell, W. (1918) A Case of Identity. Journal of the Institute of American Criminal Law and Criminology, Volume Nine. Chicago, Illinois: The Northwestern University Press.

Roswell Sturdivant (1822) Torch Light and Public Advertiser, Hagerstown Maryland, August 6, 1822.

Rothert, O. (1924) *The Outlaws of Cave-in-Rock.* Southern Illinois University Press.

Sheley-Cruz, Shalane J. (2010) A Genealogical Record of the 19th Century Cothrell Families of New York, Ohio, and Northern Indiana.

Smith, J. (1969) *Blacklegs, Regulators and the Hanging of Gregory McDougle.* Published by Attorney John Martin Smith, Auburn, Indiana.

Smith, T. (1855) *Legends of the War of Independence, and of the Earlier Settlements in the West.* Louisville, Ky.: J. F. Brennan, Publisher.

Tanner, G. (1861) *Cases Argued and Determined in the Supreme Court of Judicature of the State of Indiana. Indianapolis, Indiana:* Merrill and Company, pgs. 52-57.

The History of Linn County Iowa: containing a history of the county, its cities, and towns. (1878) Chicago: Western Historical Company.

The Noble County Regulators, A Desperado Hung (1858, February 4) *St. Joseph Valley Register*, p.3.

The Noble and Lagrange Regulators (1858, February 13) *Fort Wayne Sentinel*, p.1.

The Noble County Regulators (1858, February 6) *Fort Wayne Sentinel*, p.1.

The Regulators (1858, February 17) *Goshen Democrat*, p.1.

The Tale of Crime and Blood in Northern Indiana (1858, February 3) *Goshen Democrat*, p. 2.

The Vigilance Committee in Noble County – Man Hung! (1858, January 30) *Fort Wayne Sentinel*, p.1.

Topeka Area Historical Society (2011) *The Blacklegs, the Regulators and the Hanging*. Volume 4, Number 3, July – September 2011 Edition.

Townsend: His Career and Trial at Cayuga. (1857) Narrative of the life of the daring murderer, highwayman, & burglar, William Townsend. Digitized by the University of Alberta Libraries, on file with the National Archives, Washington DC.

Transactions of the Illinois State Historical Society For the Year 1906. (1906) Springfield"
Illinois State Journal Co. State Printers.

Trial of One Hundred and Twelve Men for Murder (1841) Schenectady New York
Cabinet, p.2.

Troyer, H. (1950) *The Salt and the Savor.* New York: A.A. Wyn Publishers.

Valparaiso University Law Review (1997) *The Patriot Movement: Refreshing the Tree of
Liberty with Fertilizer Bombs and the Blood of Martyrs.* Valparaiso, Indiana: Valparaiso
University Law Review & Thompson Smith.

Waddell, R. (1920), *History of northeast Indiana: Lagrange, Steuben, Noble and Dekalb
Counties,* Chicago: Lewis Pub. Co., 1,230 pgs., pgs. 319 – 324.

Wellman, P. (1964) *Spawn of Evil: The Invisible Empire of Soulless Men which for a
Generation Held the Nation in a Spell of Terror* W. Foulsham & Co Ltd Publishing
Company. Virginia: Double Day Publishing.

Whittet, R. (1914) Pioneer Annals, Township of Moore: The Missouri, Illinois and Eastern Trading Company. Brigden, Ontario: Progress .

Wood, W. & Gray, W. (1851) *Report of the Great Conspiracy Case.* Detroit: Advertiser and Free Press.

Would Die, But Not Confess: Two Indiana Men Whom Lynchers Couldn't Terrify (1902, July 4) *The Sun of New York*, p.1.

Wyatt, K. (2012) *Peek Through Time: Jackson County farmers tried for burning Michigan Central Railroad depot.* Jackson Citizen Patriot, February 22, 2012.

SPECIAL THANKS:

Allen County Public Library, Fort Wayne, Indiana

Ancestry.com

Angela Mapes Turner (family of Arthur F. Mapes)

Attorney John Martin Smith (and family) of Auburn, Indiana

Attorney Thompson Smith of Auburn, Indiana

Barbara Thornton, Wallaceburg, Ontario

Ben Schopeski

Carnegie Public Library of Steuben County

Chicago Historical Society, Chicago, Illinois

Christine Pellor

Canadian Historian and Author Ed Butts

Chatham This Week, Chatham, Ontario

Dalonda Young, Lagrange County GIS

273

Fort Wayne Journal Gazette

George Brown of the Clermont Sun, Batavia, Ohio

Hancock-Findlay Public Library

Illinois State Historical Society

Indiana Historical Society, Indianapolis, Indiana

Indiana State Digital Archives

Iowa State Historical Society

Jackson Citizen Patriot, Jackson, Michigan

Janet Sweeney, Stones Trace Historical Society

Historian J. Thomas Kerr, Ontario

Katie Erickson

Kentucky Historical Society

Lafayette Historical Society, Lafayette, Ohio

Lagrange County GIS

Lagrange Historical Society, Lagrange, Indiana

Lagrange Standard

Library of Canada and Archives

Library of Congress, Washington D.C.

Megan Rachelle Shufelt, Ball State University

My Family

National Archives and Records Administration

New York Times Company

Ohio Historical Society

Old Stone House Museum of Butler, Pennsylvania

Ontario Genealogical Society

Paquette Family of Western Pennsylvania

Probst Family Farm, Bluffton, Ohio

Professor Michael Lewis, Tiffin University

Rita Lehner, Lagrange County GIS

Shalane J. Sheley-Cruz

Slippery Rock University, Pennsylvania

Special Agent in Charge Chad Saunders, US Office of Personnel Management

Special Agent in Charge Nathan Allen, US Office of Personnel Management

St. Joseph County Historical Society, Centreville, Michigan

Stone's Trace Historical Society, Ligonier, Indiana

Sue Cox of the Latta Genealogical Society

Summit County Historical Society, Akron, Ohio

The Church of Jesus Christ of Latter-Day Saints

Toledo Blade, Toledo, Ohio

Topeka Historical Society, Topeka, Indiana

United States Marshal Service Public Affairs Office

United States Secret Service Public Affairs Office

Wallaceburg Historical Museum, Wallaceburg, Ontario

Wayne Demunn

Zipper City Photography

I will beg forgiveness of anyone else who I may have forgotten to include!

And a special thanks to the Regulators, Blacklegs, and those from the 1800's who

documented their history

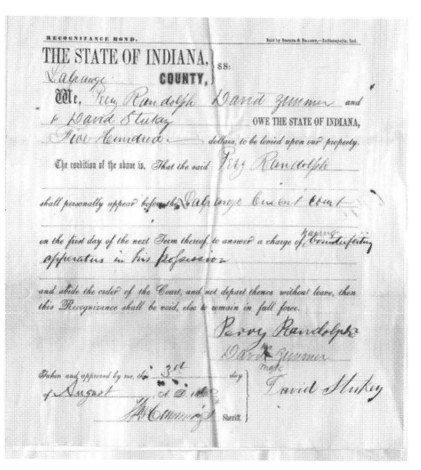

Recognizance bond paperwork for Perry Randolph and associates from LaGrange Circuit Court from August 3, 1860, signed by Sheriff William Cummings. (courtesy of Lagrange GIS)

Roster of the Regulators formed at Wright Corners, Lagrange County, Indiana (courtesy of Lagrange GIS)

State of Indiana Lagrange County sct

Be it Remembered that on the twenty third day of May in the year of our Lord one thousand eight hundred and Thirty two Joel Leverich James Leverich and Moses Rice personally appeared before me Ephraim Sely a Justice of the peace of said County and Jointly and Severally acknowledged themselves to owe to the State of Indiana the sum of five hundred dollars to be levied of their and each of their goods and Chattles lands and tenements if default be made in the Condition following to wit the Condition of this recconizance is such that if the ~~said~~ Joel Leverich shall personally appear at and before the next circuit Court to be holden in and for said County on the first day of the term then and there to answer said State on a complaint of being guilty of pasing Counterfeit Money and aiding assisting and abetting in the Commission thereof made against him on the Oath of Joshua L Hobbs Benjamin Gale Thomas Gale Edmund Littlefield Ossa Earl William Thrall and Jacob Vandusanter and abide the Judgement of the Court thereon and not depart without leave then this recognizance to be void otherwise in full force and virtue in law — Joel Leverich
~~taken and~~ acknowledged and approved by me at the County aforesaid Moses Rice
this 23rd day of May 1832 James Leverich
Ephraim Sely J.P. [Seal]

Court paperwork from the arrest of Joel "Bogus Coon" Leverich, James Leverich, and Moses Rice from Lagrange County, Indiana in May 1832. Leverich later moved with the syndicate to Iowa (courtesy of Lagrange County GIS)

279

"The Blacklegs"
By Arthur Franklin Mapes
(reprinted with permission from Angela Mapes Turner

Ole Sassafras John lit up his pipe,
An' gazed up at the sky.
I knew 'at he wus dreamin' up
A tale of days gone by.

I scooted over by his side
As quiet as could be,
Fer I liked to hear the stories
'at ole John would spin fer me.

He told about the settlers
Of the Indiana hills,
Of wagon trains, an' Indian trails,
An' creakin' water mills.

He remembered when the stagecoach
Rumbled down the ole plank road,
An' how a yoke of oxen
Could pull a heavy load.

He talked about the cabin loft
Where he would lay an' dream,
An' seemed as tho' he still could see
The tallow candles gleam.

'Twus the days when Greg McDougal
Led his darin' Blackleg band
Until the Regulators
Rose in strength to take a hand.

In the village, known as Northport,
Greg McDougal's cabin stood.
He wus crooked like an ole rail fence,
But folks thought he wus good.

He would go to church on Sunday,
An' would join in prayer an' song,
But jist when folks would turn their backs
He'd allus do 'em wrong.

His gang would kill an' plunder,
Strikin' almost every place,
Then would vanish in the forest
An' never leave a trace.

Then the Regulators gathered
Down at Col. Cochran's Inn,
An' vowed the Blacklegs had to pay
Fer every crime an' sin.

They circled 'round by Northport,
Down to Kendallville an' back,
They searched the gloomy forests
An' the bogs of tamarack.

They caught up with the Blacklegs,
An' at last the truth came out,
An' the pious Greg McDougal
His innocence did shout;

But the justice of the settlers
Wus strong, an' swift, an' sure,
Fer the plague 'at had beset 'em
There was jist one simple cure.

So a caravan of wagons
Took the road to Diamond Lake.
The men had jist one purpose,
McDougal's life to take.

The sky looked dark an' stormy,
Yet the wind seemed sad an' still,
When they strung up Greg
McDougal
Frum a tree on Diamond Hill.

They buried him at Northport
Where his gravestone can be seen,
An' old an' dated slab of gray
Above the grass of green.

There's a moral to this story
'at ole Sassafras has told,
"Don't ever git to cravin'
Fer another feller's gold,

'Tis better to be down an' out,
An' have a mind 'ats free,
Than to end up like McDougal
Hangin' frum a big oak tree."

This page intentionally left blank

Made in the USA
Charleston, SC
09 March 2015